*Canoeing
Central
New York*

Canoeing Central New York

DR. WILLIAM P. EHLING

Photographs by the Author

Backcountry Publications, Inc.
Woodstock, Vermont

Invitation to the reader Rivers and creeks are particularly given to altering their courses of travel; and with time, roads and bridges, access points and landmarks also undergo alteration. If you find that changes have occurred on the waterways described in this book, please let the author and publisher know so that corrections can be made in future editions. Other comments and suggestions for additional river trips also are welcome. Address all correspondence to:
Editor, Canoeing
Backcountry Publications, Inc.
P.O. Box 175
Woodstock, VT 05091

©1982 by William P. Ehling
All rights reserved
Published by Backcountry Publications Inc.
Woodstock, Vermont 05091

Printed in the United States of America
Design by Wladislaw Finne

Library of Congress Cataloging in Publication Data

Ehling, William P., 1920-
   Canoeing central New York.

   1. Canoes and canoeing—New York (State)—Guide-books.
2. Outdoor recreation—New York (State)—Guide-books.
3. Family recreation—New York (State)—Guide-books.
4. New York (State)—Description and travel—1981-
—Guide-books. I. Title.
GV776.N7E35   917.47   82-4018
ISBN 0-942440-01-3 (pbk.)   AACR2

Maps drawn by Richard Widhu
Cover photograph by Stan Phaneuf

Second printing 1987

To my children, Terry Ann, Clare Mare, and James Philip, with whom I shared the outdoors when they were young and who, on the morrow, may pass on to friends and children their findings and feelings about the world of nature; and to Olga whose love of the outdoors and constant wonder about and appreciation for the woods and fields, hills and streams, plantlife and birdlife has made every trip a joyful adventure.

Acknowledgments   Many thanks to members of the Ka-Na-Wa-Ke Canoe Club of Syracuse with whom I have often canoed on club outings, and from whom I have learned much about the way of the canoe. It was on these outings that I became familiar with many of the attractive streams that flow in central New York. I am especially indebted to the people who served as my canoe partners, not only on club trips, but on the many reconnaissance missions run on scores of streams which eventually were described in this book. My sincerest thanks go to Brian Simson, Olga Stirpe, and William Thayer whose companionship and good humor made every trip a memorable one and, in a very real sense, made this book possible. My thanks also go to my editor, Susan Edwards, who gave generously of her time and attention to see that the copy was accurate and readable and whose many suggestions were most helpful and much appreciated.

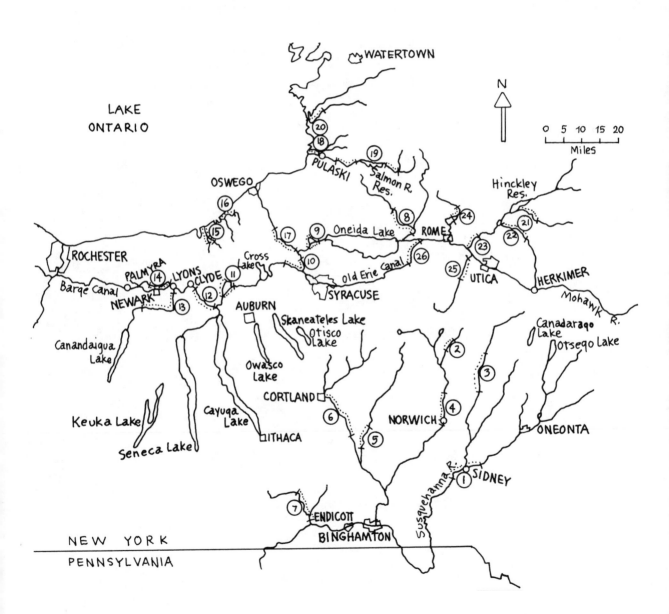

Contents

Introduction

The lure of moving water is hard to resist. For some canoeists it is simply a desire to float the quiet water of a lazy stream; for others it is the urge to run water that rips and roars—the whitewater or even wildwater of an untamed river. But one thing appears certain: once you have felt your canoe responding to a stream's current you'll never be the same again.

Canoeing changes people in wonderful ways. It strengthens the muscles and sharpens the senses. It brings out the adventurer, the voyageur, in each of us. It can give a person a never-ending itch to see backcountry and wilderness that can only be reached by canoe. It can turn paddlers, sometimes when they least expect it, into poets.

Sensitive to the ways in which canoeing can fine tune a paddler's ear, Thomas F. Waters, in *The Streams and River of Minnesota,* speaks reverently of the sounds of a river's passage, but he notes that "sounds of streams and river bottoms are not confined to this music," for there are also, "the symphony of bird songs, buzzing of insects, croaking of amphibians, the whistle and sigh of down-canyon winds in the treetops"—all these sounds make up "the treasure of any quietwater stretches."'

Another writer who has been able to capture in poetic words the appeal of canoeing is Sigurd F. Olson. In his *Wilderness Days* he says, "There is magic in the feel of a paddle and movement of a canoe, a magic compounded of distance, adventure, solitude, and peace. The way of the canoe is the way of the wilderness and of a freedom almost forgotten."

And even more poignantly, Olson adds, "When man is part of his canoe, he is part of what canoes have ever known"—the waterways of ages past and of a special way of life that returns like the renewing freshness and beauty of a new spring.

This book is intended for those who are, or who aspire to be, canoeists—for those who enjoy water travel under their own power, where movement is muscle-generated, not motor-induced, and where the only man-made sounds are the dipping of a paddle and the lapping of a bow's parting waves.

For *aficionados* of canoe and paddle, central New York's array of streams provides locales for sport and recreation—creeks and rivers ranging from quietwater to whitewater. Here a paddler can acquire the skills of a good canoeist, or refine skills already acquired.

Central New York
Location
and Waterways

No definitive boundaries set off central New York from the rest of the state. New York's govermental departments have their own ways of subdividing the state to fit specific administrative needs, resulting in several different state-designated "central New York" regions.

However, if you draw a 75-mile circle around the city of Syracuse you have what most people think of as central New York. This circle runs above Watertown in the north, just beyond Little Falls in the east, below Binghamton in the south, and just touching Rochester in the west.

The creeks and rivers covered in this book are within this approximately 3,600-square mile area. The settings for the described trips are predominately rural; however, various portions of a stream may range from wild to urban. An effort has been made to identify the unusual geological, ecological and various man-made features which distinguish each trip.

Central New Yorkers are blessed with an abundant supply of waterways, ranging from small creeks to broad rivers, and from streams that rush and tumble down craggy slopes to those which meander slowly and idly through flat, green valleys. Over a hundred streams in central New York are canoeable. This book treats less than a third of them. We hope the reader has an opportunity to take not only the 26 trips described here, but to paddle many of the other waters as well.

Watersheds and Flows

In central New York, creeks and rivers run in all directions, to make up several different flows and watersheds. More specifically, the streams in this region drain into four watersheds—the Susquehanna River watershed (south flow), the Finger Lakes-Oneida Lake watershed (central flow), the Lake Ontario-St. Lawrence watershed (north flow), and the Mohawk watershed (east flow). Water from the streams in the central flow eventually feeds into Lake Ontario via the Oswego River, to become part of the north flow.

As the Table of Contents shows, the waterways featured in this book are grouped into these four watersheds, with an almost equal number falling in each flow area.

Lands and Landforms

The lands in central New York are quite varied. Nonetheless, the region can be divided into several geographic areas—the Ontario lowlands, the Appalachian highlands, and the Mohawk Valley. The first borders Lake Ontario, extending inland from the lake ten to thirty miles; streams found here generally flow northward into the lake. The second is found in the southern half of the upstate region; most of the streams here flow southward, with the remainder flowing northward into the Mohawk River. The third area is the broad flatland which drains the Appalachian highlands to the south and the Adirondack foothills to the north.

Within these areas, the landforms range from flat marshy sections to an undulating landscape made up of small hills called drumlins, and from deep, gorge-like valleys in a wilderness setting to wide, even valleys between low, forested hills in which are found the croplands and pasturelands of prosperous farm communities.

The Ontario lowland and Appalachian highland areas are further divided geologically and geographically. The lowland area includes from west to east: the Ontario Drumlin region, the Ontario Ridge and Swampland region, the Eastern Ontario Hill region, and the Oneida Plain region. The highland area within central New York is divided into the Susquehanna Hill region and the Finger Lakes region. Running along an east-west axis between the Oneida Plain region on the west and the Hudson Valley region on the east is the Mohawk Valley region.

Geology and Glaciation   The landscape surrounding central New York's canoeable streams has been shaped by two processes—the slow geological process of sedimentation and uplifts, and the glaciation effects of invading and retreating glaciers. The former is a building-up process—it has given us the sedimentary rocks of limestone and shale found in the central region, the sandstone in the northern part, and the uplifted hills in the south. The latter wears down and scours—it has given us the rounded hills, U-shaped valleys, hanging streams, valley-headed moraines, kames, eskers, drumlins, kettle lakes, and valleys filled with glacial drift and till.

When the glaciers melted back during the Pleistocene epoch some 12,000 years ago, the meltwaters flowing along the glacier-deepened valleys ate their way through shale and limestone to produce many of our presentday stream systems, such as those of the Tioughnioga River, the Otselic River, the Mohawk River, and Oriskany Creek.

Canoes and Canoeing
The Canoe

The modern canoe is a remarkable craft. It incorporates the latest in chemistry and technology, giving us first the aluminum, and now the fiberglass, A.B.S. (Acrylonitrile-Butadiene-Styrene), and Kevlar canoes. Today we speak generally of recreational and racing canoes, but the low, lean look of the racing canoe has increasingly been incorporated into the design of most modern recreational canoes.

Still, the basic design has remained relatively unchanged, coming down to us through the centuries from the Indian's birchbark canoe. Here was a craft which the white man quickly adopted as his principal mode of transportation to and through the American western wilderness.

Two of the qualities that make the canoe a remarkable craft are durability and practicality. A lot of punishment can be inflicted on the modern canoe and still it will last through several owners. It is eminently practical—easy to store, transport, and carry.

It is an extremely maneuverable craft. In the hands of an expert running whitewater or shooting rapids, the canoe's instant responsiveness to every move is thrilling.

It is also one of the most versatile means of recreation in the world. The canoe can be paddled, poled, or, with a few additions, sailed. It can be propelled in quietwater, fastwater, and, with a cover, in whitewater and even in wildwater. It can be shot through rapids or surfed on ocean waves. It can be moved through long river systems and over vast oceans. Men have paddled canoes incredible distances—down the Mississippi, along the eastern United States' inland waterway, through the Caribbean Sea and the Gulf of Mexico, and from the Arctic Circle down Canada's many waterways to the Great Lakes. In this book waterways have been described in which all three types of propulsion —paddling, poling, and sailing—are possible.

For many, of course, canoe paddling is an end to be pursued for its own delights. But canoeing can also serve in an auxiliary relationship, to be enjoyed along with other activities, such as fishing and birding, day-tripping or weekend outings, back country treks and wilderness camping. These possibilities were also kept in mind when the trips were selected.

Canoeing Competence

Perhaps to a casual observer canoeing looks simple, but there is more to it than jumping into a canoe and thrusting a paddle into the water. Canoeing is learned, and it should be learned under qualified instruction. No one interested in the streams in this book ought to take to a canoe without having first completed a basic course. Call your local American Red Cross chapter to find one.

Even flatwater canoeing requires the mastery of beginning skills; without these, canoeing can easily become a fatiguing and sometimes painful chore in which distaste soon replaces enjoyment. As the water speeds and starts to race the skill requirements become more demanding, but with that speed and demand come new excitement and pleasure.

Your competence as a paddler can be rated on a scale running from I to V:

I. Beginner: One who knows the basic strokes and is able to paddle in either the bow or stern position in flatwater.

II. Novice: One who has some competence in some of the whitewater strokes such as high and low brace, who knows how to read water, and who knows how to negotiate easy, regular rapids.

III. Intermediate: One who has mastered the ability to negotiate higher rapids—Class II water—requiring several maneuvers and different strokes, and who knows how to make eddy turns in fast water in either the bow or stern position.

IV. Advanced or Expert: One who has the ability to run difficult—Class IV—rapids in either the bow or stern position, and who has experienced running and maneuvering in heavy water.

V. Leader: One who is an expert canoeist with experience and training to lead groups that include people with varying skills and competence on different kinds of navigable water.

Rating the Stream

Along with assuming basic canoeing competence, this book assumes that its readers will properly match their competence to the difficulty of the streams. Many of these rivers and creeks can be paddled by beginners and novices; others require the paddling skills of intermediate canoeists; and a few of the faster waterways, especially if they are canoed in early spring, demand the skills of advanced or expert canoeists.

The American Whitewater Affiliation (AWA) Safety Code lists six *classes*:

Class I. Easy: Essentially stillwater or slow moving water with clear passages, light riffles, occasional bends and slow turns. Bridge piers the most difficult obstacle encountered.

Class II. Medium Difficult: Easy-to-regular rapids with waves up to 3 feet, wide, clear channels, moderate current between rocks and over low steps or ledges.

Class III. Moderately Difficult: Rapids are high with irregular waves capable of swamping a canoe; channels are clear but narrow, frequently filled with rocks; requiring expert skill and tricky maneuvering. Rapids may require scouting from shore.

Class IV. Difficult: Rapids are long, powerful, and difficult with large standing waves and souse holes; such sections cannot be run with an open canoe.

Those who use covered canoes and kayaks should be master of the Eskimo roll.

The next two classes, Class V (Extremely Difficult) and Class VI (Extraordinarily Difficult) cover violent and extremely turbulent water with swift and dangerous currents, and in case of the latter class the water is nearly impossible and always dangerous to run.

If the water temperature is below 50°F., or if your trip is an extended one into a wilderness area, the stream should be considered one class more difficult than usual.

During late spring or early summer, when the water level is between medium and medium high, the streams in this book fall into the first two classes. During the early spring runoffs many of them become Class III waterways.

Beginner and novice canoeists should stay on Class I water. To encounter a stream with Class II rapids, the paddler should have intermediate canoeing skill.

Water Level

One of the primary factors determining a stream's classification is the water level. As the water level changes so do the stream's characteristics and, hence, its rating. A Class II stream can turn into a Class IV stream when the water is unusually high, and a springtime Class IV stream can become a Class I stream when water levels drop to low in midsummer.

The International Rating System classifies water levels as low, medium, medium high, high, high-high, and flood. The ideal water levels for most canoeists are those falling into the medium and medium high categories. Medium means normal level and flow, good canoeing conditions. At medium high the water level and flow is slightly above normal, with water extending up to the vegetation on the banks, giving the best level for navigating the stream's more difficult sections. At higher levels the water becomes turbulent (called "heavy" water), contains powerful currents with complex and dangerous hydraulics, and should be canoed, if canoed at all, only by experts.

Readers should remember that streams not only change their characteristics en route, but they frequently alter their natures from one season to the next. A waterway that is low and gentle in midsummer may have been wildly turbulent and even dangerous for an expert the previous spring. Even in summer an intense rain can bring a stream up from one to three feet within a 24-hour period, changing its personality dramatically.

Controlling Conditions

You don't have to be a scientist to plan a successful canoe outing, but it helps to know something about the meterological, climatological, and topographical factors that affect water flows and stream levels. It is important to know something about man-made factors as well, including locations of dams, water control gates, canal locks, and times of water releases.

Meterological factors include precipitation (snow and rain), temperature, and transpiration. In central New York snow varies from extremely high (over 300 inches per year) in the northern section (especially in the Tug Hill region) to moderate and low as one moves southward. Temperature is important in early spring; low temperatures can mean frozen ground with resulting extremely fast runoffs. As the snow cover disappears, so does the importance of temperature.

The seasonal or annual norms of precipitation, temperature, and transpiration constitute the climatological factors. In central New York rainy periods are frequent in spring, less so in summer. In general there is more rain in autumn than in summertime. A good rule of thumb to remember is that water levels vary with the leaves on the trees. With the emergence of leaves in spring, the surface runoffs decline substantially (rainy periods decrease, the ground becomes drier, and consumption of water by all plants increases sharply); with the turning of leaves in the fall the water levels rise (for the opposite reasons).

Topographical features also control water levels. Streams and rivers flowing down escarpments or steep-sided hills quickly fill with snow meltwaters or rain runoffs, making waterways rise rapidly; they can drop just as quickly. In contrast, waterways flowing through flatter terrain flanked by tree-covered hills collect meltwater or rain water more slowly, maintaining an above-normal level of water for long periods and extending these streams' runability.

March through May, when the water levels are up, creeks and rivers all over central New York are runable; but by midsummer, fastwater streams with easy rapids usually require medium or medium high water levels for good passage.

Water levels of two rivers described in this book are regulated by water releases used to generate hydroelectric power. On both the Salmon River and West Canada Creek, water is released by Niagara Mohawk Power Corporation, with the release times usually determined by power consumption periods and by the amount of water in the upstream dams.

Canoeing Hazards

Even if you are a competent canoeist you still face hazards in canoeing —threats to life which should not be minimized. And there are quite a few possible hazards—starting with high water, turbulent rapids, and standing waves high enough to swamp a canoe.

In early spring or early winter cold water is one of the canoeist's greatest dangers. Any water below 50°F is *cold,* and in 33°F a person can survive for only five or ten minutes. Two recommendations suffice: avoid icy water or, if you must canoe on such water, wear a wet suit.

Early spring produces not only icy water from snow meltwaters but also flood or near-flood conditions. This water may look tempting, but where there is pitch to the stream the waters contain powerful, often violent, and always dangerous currents.

Another danger lies in souse holes and reversals, found below heavy rapids or dams where the water forms whirlpools or rolls back upstream. Once you are caught in one of these, you and your canoe are tumbled over and over, and it is almost impossible to break out of the water's grip. The best course of action is to carry around such danger spots.

Strainers are often found on streams, nearly always around a sharp bend. They are any collection of debris—pilings, brush, logs, downed trees —through which water can pass, but which is capable of catching and pinning a canoe or a person. A powerful fastwater current can make efforts to dislodge an entrapped canoe nearly hopeless, and the suction created in such situations can pull and trap a canoeist underwater.

Still another serious problem is barbed wire. In early spring barbed wire fences crossing streams are usually washed out, but by May farmers have repaired their fences and barbed wire is again across the streams, not always where it was before. Streams which had none last year may have some this year. The wire is hard to see. Keep an eye out for fence posts on the edge of the stream.

Rock gardens and boulders can also be hazardous in fastwater. Powerful currents can smash a canoe against a rock and hold it there. Aluminum canoes can literally be bent around a boulder. Once pinned to a large rock, a canoe may be pried loose only with considerable help and labor.

The rule in dangerous situations is simple: always back away from trouble. Your canoeing course taught you how to back paddle—make use of that stroke when hazards appear.

How to Use This Book   On the top righthand side of each writeup's first page is a brief summary of that stream's described trip—the put-in and take-out spots, the trip's length in miles, and the skill level that canoeists should have achieved to canoe this portion of the stream at low, medium, or medium-high water.

Additional information about each waterway is summarized in the table below the trip summary. Included here are the principal access spots to be found on the stream's canoeable sections, the interval distance between these spots, the drop in feet and the gradient (feet/mile) for each interval distance, trip time in hours for each interval, water conditions, and any obstacles.

The run-down of access points offers an overview of the stream's entire canoeable area, with information pertaining to the suggested trip printed in italics. The drop and gradient tell the canoeist at a glance what kind of water he or she is facing—whether, for example, this river would be too flat or too fast.

The figures in the table are estimates, some more exact than others. The

interval distances are quite accurate, but the trip times are approximations which can vary with water conditions, the paddling ability of the canoeists, their speed of travel, and the length of sightseeing pauses.

At the bottom of the table are a list of USGS (United States Geological Survey) maps covering all of the waterway's territory from origin to terminus (or, as in the case of the Susquehanna River, the part of the river that lies in New York State). With one exception, all these maps are from the 7.5-minute series; in the list given for Black Creek, one is a 15-minute map. The names of the maps that relate to the suggested trip are printed in italics.

A simplified map accompanies each writeup, giving principal roads near or crossing the stream, the recommended start and end spots for the described trip, alternate put-in and take-out sites, and other pertinent information such as location of dams and locks and the names of towns and villages.

Each writeup is divided into five sections beginning with a general introduction to the stream and its environment, followed by a section marked *Access* in which routes to the take-out and put-in sites are designated. Next comes a section titled *The Creek,* or *The River* with more detailed information about the waterway's salient attributes—origin, location, direction of flow, length, and setting. Then comes *The Trip* section in which the stream's features (rapids, drops, etc.) and surrounding landscape encountered en route are chronologically highlighted. Finally there is a section on *Alternate Canoe Routes,* containing suggestions about other portions of the stream and nearby creeks or rivers which you may wish to canoe in addition to the described trip.

*Susquehanna
Watershed
(South Flow)*

1

Susquehanna River (Middle)

Described Trip:
Unadilla to Bainbridge
9 miles
Novice at medium water
Intermediate at medium high water

Access Points	Interval Distance	Drop and (Gradient)	Trip Time	Water Conditions	Obstacles
Otsego Lake at Cooperstown					
	14 miles	44' (3)	5 hrs.	Moderate	Dam
Jct. Cherry Valley Creek at Milford					
	12	10' (1)	4	Flat	None
Good Year Lake					
	2	30' (0)	¾	Moderate	Dam
Jct. Schenevus Creek at Colliersville					
	8½	20' (3)	3	Moderate	Dam
Oneonta					
	9¼	40' (4)	4	Moderate	None
Otego					
	6½	20' (3)	2¼	Moderate	None
Wells Bridge					
	6	20' (3)	2	Moderate	None
Jct. Ouleout Creek					
	1½	20' (10)		Moderate	Dam
Unadilla					
	5¼	9' (2)	2	*Moderate*	*None*
Sidney					
	1	1' (1)	½	*Moderate*	*None*
Jct. Unadilla River					
	4¼	50' (10)	1½	*Moderate*	*None*
Bainbridge					
	4½	5' (1)	1½	Flat	None
Afton					
	25½	60' (2)	9	Flat	None
Pennsylvania State Line					
	28	73' (3)	10	Flat	Dam
Jct. Chenango River at Binghamton					
	23	34' (1)	8	Flat	3 dams
Owego					
	23	52' (2)	8	Flat	None
Jct. Chemung River at Tiogo Point					

USGS (7.5') Maps: Cooperstown, Milford, West Davenport, Oneonta, Otego, Franklin, Unadilla, Sidney, North Sanford, Afton, Windsor, Gulf Summit, Binghamton East, Binghamton West, Endicott, Apalachin, Owego, Barton; in Pa.: Great Bend, Susquehanna.

The Susquehanna River's reputation begins with its length. After the St. Lawrence River, the Susquehanna has the largest watershed system of any river in the eastern United States, flowing 420 miles from its source at Otsego Lake in central New York, south through Pennsylvania and Maryland, to empty into the Chesapeake Bay.

It is the main water artery of central New York's south flow, collecting water from more than a dozen rivers and streams, including such canoeable waters as Cherry Valley Creek, Schenevus Creek, Charlotte Creek, Otego Creek, Unadilla River (see Trip 3), Chenango River (see Trip 4), Otselic River (see Trip 5), Tioughnioga River (see Trip 6), Owego and Catatonk Creeks (see Trip 7), Apalachin Creek, Cayuta Outlet, and Chemung River. The list makes an impressive watershed family.

It was because of this watershed's extensive character that the early fur traders from the Mohawk Valley were able to deal with Indians as far south as Pennsylvania. Later, as upstate New York became settled, lumber and farm products were floated downriver on rafts to markets as distant as Harrisburg and Baltimore.

General James Clinton assured the Susquehanna's place in the early history of this country by a daring exploit which began on Otsego Lake, and ended 172 miles downstream in Pennsylvania. A plan formulated during the Revolutionary War called for three Colonial divisions to be assembled at Tiogo Point (near Athens, Pennsylvania) under the command of General John Sullivan. Their orders were to attack and subdue several Iroquois tribes in central New York's Finger Lakes Region who were loyal to the British, and secure America's western flank by destroying the Indians' villages, croplands, and stored food.

General Clinton brought his troops from Albany to Otsego Lake, where his men built 220 bateaux (light, flat-bottomed boats), and a three-foot-high dam at the lake's outlet. Then they waited for the lake to rise.

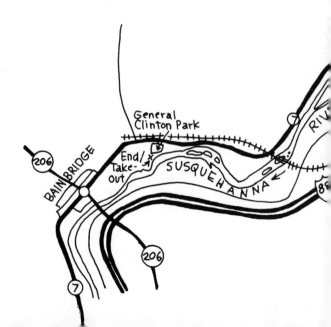

On August 9, 1779, the dam was smashed and the fleet of bateaux—carrying 1,800 men and supplies—surged downstream on the crest of a man-made flood. By this means General Clinton's forces reached Tiogo Point, where they joined the other troops of General Sullivan for the campaign into upstate New York.

Today the name of General Clinton is still heard along the Susquehanna, but now it is in connection with the General Clinton Canoe Regatta which features, among other races, the famous 70-mile World Championship Flatwater Endurance Race from the Otsego Lake outlet at Cooperstown to Bainbridge's General Clinton Park. Hundreds of paddlers participate in the three-day event, which is held each year on Memorial Day weekend, and is billed as the largest regatta of its kind in the world.

Access For the most part, paved highways run along both sides of the river. From Cooperstown to Oneonta the main highway is NY 28, and from Oneonta to Harpursville it is NY 7; while the route from Harpursville to the Pennsylvania state line is NY 79, and thereafter it is PA 92.

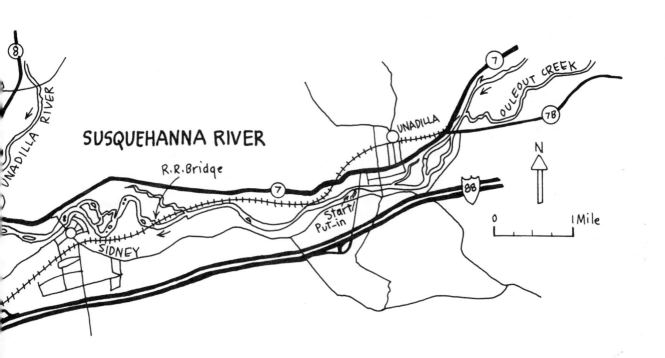

For the suggested trip the take-out point is General Clinton Park on the east side of Bainbridge, off NY 7. The park abuts the river, and ample parking space is available there.

The put-in is the fishing access area on the south side of the river at Unadilla. It can be reached from either NY 7 or I-88. A short carry from the parking lot brings you to the river's edge.

The River

The Susquehanna forms the southern boundary of what the state identifies in its tourist literature as the Leatherstocking Country made famous by James Fenimore Cooper, particularly by the writer's *Leatherstocking Tales,* whose heroes struggled to open up the new land that surrounded "Glimmerglass Lake" (Otsego Lake).

New York's portion of the Susquehanna can be divided into an upper section from Otsego Lake to Goodyear Lake (a dammed portion just north of Colliersville), a middle section from Goodyear Lake to Windsor, and a lower portion from Windsor to the Pennsylvania state line, south of Waverly.

Unlike many other rivers, this one is canoeable from its very beginning to its end; so you can start anywhere you wish and canoe as far as your inclination and endurance allow—into the Atlantic Ocean, if you so desire.

After the spring runoff (when the river can rise as much as seven feet in its lower reaches), the Susquehanna is a gentle river. For almost its entire length in New York its gradient averages about 3, indicating that this is water that beginner and novice canoeists can manage without difficulty.

Goodyear Lake is large enough to permit excellent canoe sailing. North of this lake the river is quite flat. Because of the way the dam backs up the water here, the river can be canoed upstream almost as easily as downstream. Below the dam, however, the river becomes more lively, and the current is noticeable, steady, and strong enough to make upstream paddling exceedingly difficult. Hence, from Goodyear Lake to Afton the paddler enjoys moderately fast water. Thereafter, the river broadens and slows to flatwater.

Conveniently, islands—some with and some without trees—are found scattered throughout the river's length, providing ideal locations for lunch breaks. About every quarter mile you will encounter a nice run. The runs are marked by riffles or small standing waves as the water speeds up over a low drop. All this makes paddling easy, and the cruising speed just right (about four miles per hour) for a day's trip.

If you can manage it, try the suggested route the day after a rain. The river should rise from six inches to a foot, and the current should increase a bit in velocity, adding to your cruising speed and making the runs even more fun.

The Trip
Start/Unadilla fishing access area

At your launch point the river is fairly wide, allowing you to set your canoe into shallow water. As you push downstream the trees along the river quickly blot out the village houses behind you.

While the river is about four canoe lengths wide in this section, it is not deep. Late in summer, when the river's level drops, you can expect to run into shallows that may even require you to get out and drag your canoe a short distance.

About 1½ miles downstream you pass your first small island, and a mile

Heading downstream on the Susquehanna.

farther you pass under a railroad bridge. Immediately beyond, there is a fairly large island on your left. From your put-in to this point the river has been attractively tree-lined, without any signs of civilization.

A mile downstream lies Sidney, but before getting there you pass a couple more islands before the river breaks up, with a smaller segment wandering off to your right and then returning to the main branch. While you can run any of three available channels here, the one on your left is the wider and deeper. In this section you will encounter some bends and fast-flowing water.

As you come out of this stretch you notice houses peeking through trees on the left bank, the first signs of Sidney. Although you continue seeing houses for a while, you are hardly aware that you are passing a fairly sizeable community. Sidney's shopping center is located well to the south of the river.

Ahead is a substantial tree-covered island. A short distance beyond is another, and as you pass this island you reach the confluence of the Unadilla flowing in from the right. This adds both water and speed to the Susquehanna as you canoe under a bridge that leads to I-88 and past a fishing access area on the right.

You notice that the river is widening. As you paddle the next three miles you also notice the current slowing just a trifle. To your right and left you can see forested hills about a quarter mile from the river's edge. Trees still line the banks, but more sparsely than before, allowing you to see some fields. A mile downstream you come to another island cluster, and a mile beyond this you encounter a series of three more islands. The banks are becoming a bit high;

End/General Clinton Park

then ahead on your right you see the park's recreation building, your take-out spot. A fairly steep but short climb brings you to the park road and your vehicle.

Alternate Canoe Routes

The Susquehanna offers the canoeist a number of excellent stretches. One starts at the outlet in Cooperstown and runs the 14-mile upper portion to the bridge that is east of Milford and immediately north of the river's junction with Cherry Valley Creek. Another section is the 12-mile flatwater stretch from Milford to Goodyear Lake. It is a little over 15 miles from Oneonta to Wells Bridge, a good day's cruise.

A nice weekend trip is the 22½-mile stretch from Wells Bridge to Afton. This, of course, includes the 10½-mile section from Unadilla to Bainbridge. Camping or motel accommodations can be found along the way.

Also, try the lower sections of the Susquehanna's several tributaries —starting in the north: Oaks Creek, Cherry Valley Creek, Schenevus Creek, Charlotte Creek, Otego Creek, and Ouleout Creek.

2

Sangerfield River

Described Trip:
Wickwire Road to Swamp Road and back
9 miles
Novice at low and medium water

Access Points	Interval Distance	Drop and (Gradient)	Trip Time	Water Conditions	Obstacles
Swamp Road					
	4½ miles	*20' (4)*	*2 hours*	*Flatwater*	*None*
Wickwire Road					
	5¼	80' (15)	2½	Flatwater; riffles	None
Poolville					
	4¼	20' (5)	2	Flatwater; fastwater	None
Earlville					
	2	10' (5)	1	Flatwater	None
NY 12B Bridge					

USGS (7.5') Maps: Cassville, Oriskany Falls, Hubbardsville, Hamilton, Earlville.

When you paddle up the Sangerfield River into Ninemile Swamp you are entering a former den of outlaws, the lair of the notorious Loomis Gang, a nineteenth-century family which practiced—very successfully—horse stealing, highway robbery, counterfeiting, arson (local barn burning), and, when the occasion demanded, murder.

Unlike the short-lived outlaws of our West, this clan established and maintained a robber empire in upstate New York for almost a hundred years. Founder of the empire, George Washington Loomis, rode into Sangerfield Center in 1802, having just escaped from a Vermont posse for running stolen horses. He married in Sangerfield, and raised a pack of children who followed in their father's footsteps.

The family home was located on the valley's west side, on a knoll overlooking Ninemile Swamp; on a topo map it is marked Loomis Hill. The house and barn are gone, but down beyond the hay field is the swamp, looking virtually the same as it did when the Loomises were hiding stolen horses there, or hiding there themselves when cornered by the vigilantes.

Adding to the swamp's enchantment is the local legend that at night you can sometimes hear in the swamp ghost sounds of the past—muffled hoofs, and the neighing of horses being readied for the run into Pennsylvania and a sale to the Union Army.

The escapades of the Loomis family make fascinating reading; the best account is given by George W. Walter in his **The Loomis Gang**, published in 1953.

This local history makes Sangerfield River and Ninemile Swamp something

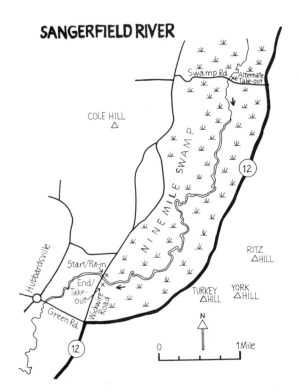

SANGERFIELD RIVER

special. Peculiarities in local terminology should also be mentioned. Ninemile Swamp really isn't nine miles long, nor is it a watery swamp. It is more like seven miles in length; and instead of a vast, soggy wetland filled with rushes and swamp weeds, it is a thickly wooded area (including some low damp spots) covered with pine, cedar, red maple, and ash—giving the valley an attractive wilderness appearance.

Then, Sangerfield River, which snakes through the swamp, might be classified by central New York standards as a creek rather than a river, although in the lower section of the swamp the waterway, while relatively narrow and slow-moving, is moderately deep.

Whether you are on a river or a creek, the four-mile trip up the Sangerfield is flat-water paddling—ideal for beginners and family groups looking for a day's outing. In good weather you will probably meet several other canoes. If you like canoe poling, the upper stretches offer an opportunity to try some snubbing (slowing the canoe with a pole when running downstream).

Access

You can locate Sangerfield River on your map by looking south of Utica. Part of the south flow drainage system, the river is a tributary of the much longer Chenango River, which it joins a mile and a half south of Earlville.

It can be reached easily via NY 12, which crosses US 20 at Sangerfield, southwest of Utica. From Sangerfield, drive south on NY 12 for 8.5 miles to an intersection marked by the presence of several nearby houses. Green Road on your right goes to Hubbardsville, just over a half mile away. At the same intersection you will find Wickwire Road running northwest. Follow this road for a little over .5 mile to where it crosses the Sangerfield River. This is both your put-in and your take-out point. There is room on both sides of the road for parking, and the river's edge is a short distance away.

The River

The headwaters of the Sangerfield are found several miles west of Ninemile Swamp, south of US 20 and north of Brookfield, high in the Susquehanna Hills. From here the water flows west and then south, as it passes through Ninemile Swamp, past Hubbardsville and Poolville, finally reaching the Chenango River south of Earlville, for a total length of 18 miles. Of these, about 9 miles are canoeable at medium water level.

Somewhat paradoxically, the most canoeable section of the river is found north of Hubbardsville, in the southern half of Ninemile Swamp. This is the river's upper section. At medium water, the lower section—from Poolville to the junction with the Chenango River—can also be paddled. At low water level, with the exception of the Ninemile Swamp section, most of Sangerfield becomes a bottom scraper and is hardly worth the effort.

In its Ninemile Swamp section, the Sangerfield has a drop of only 20 feet, making the river a flat, gentle waterway. In the Swamp Road to Chenango River section, the river has a drop of 130 feet for an overall gradient of 8.

For many canoeists, the most attractive part of Sangerfield is the Ninemile Swamp section. Here you see low, forested hills gently rolling away from the narrow valley. The swamp, uninhabited by people and untouched by civilization, is a birdwatcher's paradise—the home and refuge of hundreds of species, from the great horned owl to the marsh wren.

Getting ready to put in on the Sangerfield River.

Below the swamp the land is hilly, with much of the farming confined to narrow valleys. The population is thin and is concentrated in small villages.

The Trip
Start/Wickwire Road bridge

Launching is easy at Wickwire Road, but the stream looks discouragingly shallow here; you may even scrape bottom as you move upstream. You wonder whether this really is a canoeable stream. Suddenly the stream deepens, and remains deep for almost all of the trip upstream.

Running a total of eight miles, this up-and-back trip should take around four hours if you are relaxed about your canoeing. If you plan to stop for lunch count on more time.

From the outset trees line both sides of the stream, and there are stretches you feel you've seen before in the Adirondacks. Within the first half mile you are on a stretch of the Sangerfield that gives you a nice head-on view of forested highlands on the valley's east side: Turkey Hill, York Hill, and Ritz Hill, each over 1,800 feet high.

Soon you enter the southern interior of Ninemile Swamp. In late spring and early summer the place is filled with the songs of warblers. Along the water's edge a solitary sandpiper keeps just ahead of your canoe. A mile upstream the vegetation thins. The forest withdraws from the banks, but only temporarily.

As you approach the two-mile mark, the stream moves to the left. Ahead of you on the west side looms the peaked ridge of Cole Hill, worth a picture. The stream now swings to the right and plunges once more into the heart of the swamp, where it heads due north.

End Wickwire Road bridge

The Sangerfield is getting narrower and shallower, but press on, for you still have a quarter mile or so before you turn and head back. If the water is a bit high (perhaps after a rain) you can pole upstream to the Swamp Road bridge. If you didn't bring your pole, reverse course and take a leisurely float downstream. Break out your binoculars and study the abundant bird population with care. On a warm sunny day the trip should be a pure delight.

Alternate Canoe Routes

In spring, when the water is high and the alders low, you can paddle or pole your canoe to Swamp Road and take out there.

Also during the spring, canoeable sections of the river can be found below Hubbardsville. Enough roads cross the river to give you several easy access points. In the southern end canoeing improves in the spring from Poolville to Earlville, and, particularly, from Earlville to NY 12B.

3

Unadilla River

Described Trip:
West Edmeston to New Berlin
13½ miles
Novice at low and medium water

Access Points	Interval Distance	Drop and (Gradient)	Trip Time	Water Conditions	Obstacles
West Winfield					
	4 miles	35' (7)	1¼ hours	Flatwater	None
Unadilla Forks					
	3¼	10' (3)	1	Flatwater	None
Leonardsville					
	5	11' (2)	1½	Flatwater	None
West Edmeston					
	8	*24' (3)*	2½	*Flatwater*	*None*
South Edmeston					
	5½	*24' (5)*	1½	*Flatwater*	*None*
New Berlin					
	11	35' (3)	3½	Flatwater	None
South New Berlin					
	9½	32' (4)	3¼	Flatwater	None
Mt. Upton					
	10½	32' (3)	3½	Flatwater	None
Jct. Susquehanna River below Sidney					

USGS(7.5') Maps: Millers Mills, West Winfield, Unadilla Forks, Brookfield, New Berlin North, New Berlin South, *Holmesville, Guilford, Sidney.*

Translated from the Indian tongue, Unadilla means "Streams Meet Here," which tells you little about the scenic quality of this most attractive waterway. "River of Willows" would be a more appropriate name, because in its upper section the banks of the Unadilla are lined with towering, majestic black willows. Many of the trees have base diameters of four or five feet.

Often the willows arch over the water from both sides, forming a canopy that runs for hundreds of yards. These stretches are always cool on a hot summer day; but, more importantly, they are esthetically pleasing, as sun rays slant through the treetops to light the interiors of the cathedral-like tunnels. There are probably more willow trees per mile along this river than there are along any other stream in central New York.

The Unadilla is gentle. You don't rush or push on this river. You float and flow instead, and as you do you have time to look about, to take in the color of the hillsides and to feel the rural quiet.

Access

The described trip is on the upper section of the Unadilla, which is found south of Utica and below US 20 on your road map. Access spots can be reached via the village of Bridgewater at the junction of US 20 and NY 8. Once in Bridgewater, turn south on NY 8, which parallels the Unadilla on the river's west side for its entire length.

The Unadilla can be divided for canoeing purposes into three sections from 18 to 22 miles in length: the upper section from West Winfield to South Edmeston, the middle section from South Edmeston to South New Berlin, and the lower section from South New Berlin to Sidney.

The described trip runs south from West Edmeston to New Berlin, 10.6 road miles below. In New Berlin, turn east onto NY 80. Just before you reach the bridge you will see a parking area for your take-out vehicle on the left side of the road, adjoining the river. The river bank is low here, making canoe handling easy.

There are a number of access spots in the upper section. The time of year or the runoff condition after a rain may determine where you decide to put in. In early season, Unadilla Forks or Leonardsville are good bets, but West Edmeston is ideal at any canoeing season.

West Edmeston sits to the east of NY 8. Just turn off the highway, cross the bridge over the Unadilla, and park a couple of hundred yards beyond. The embankment is a bit steep, but you'll encounter no real difficulty getting your canoe to the water.

The River

The headwaters of the south-flowing Unadilla are found near Oredorf's Corner, about four miles east of Millers Mills and a scant eight miles from the east-flowing Mohawk River.

The peculiar juxtaposition of these two rivers—so close together and yet flowing in different directions—is explained by land topography which was shaped by surging post-glacial meltwaters about 12,000 years ago.

As the glacier melted back across the midsection of New York State, vast quantities of water—blocked on the south by hills—began cutting a west-to-east trench from Lake Erie to what is Albany today, leaving behind a broad valley plain. Immediately south of this Mohawk Valley plain is found the

UNADILLA RIVER

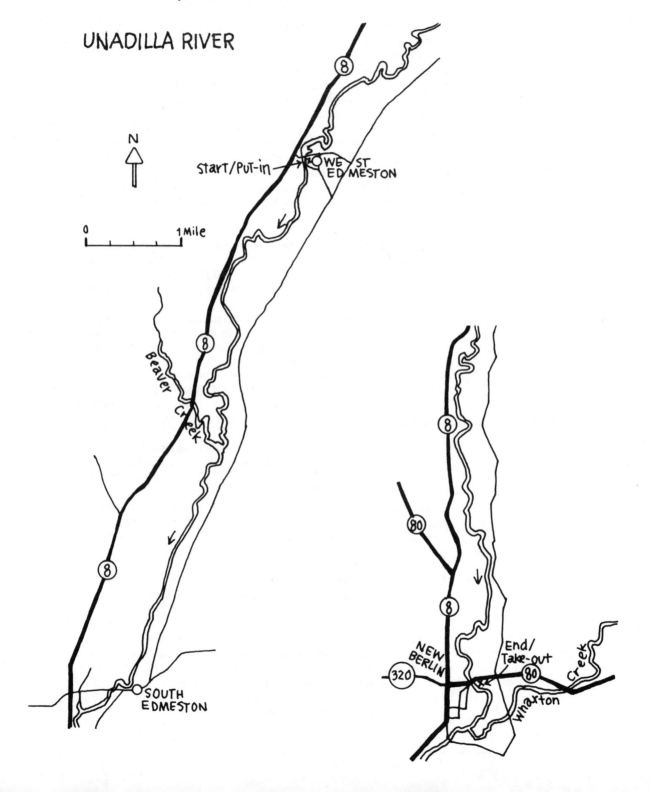

N

Start/Put-in → ⓦ WEST EDMESTON

0 1 Mile

⑧

Beaver Creek

⑧

⑧

SOUTH EDMESTON

⑧

⑧

⑧⁰

⑧

NEW BERLIN

③²⁰

End/Take-out

⑧⁰

Wharton Creek

Heading downstream on the Unadilla River.

Appalachian Highland region which directs its waters and streams southward to form the Susquehanna watershed, home of the Unadilla River.

Canoeing is a first-rate pleasure on a river as clean as the Unadilla. Its waters are almost crystal-clear for nearly two-thirds of its length. It is also virtually debris-free—there are no unsightly pileups of uprooted, dead trees and none of the human litter that usually comes from trash heaps and dumpsites often found along rivers.

The Unadilla is channeled by high, tree-lined banks. Surprisingly, the river does not undercut its banks or wash out root systems; it does not even crest its banks during the spring runoffs. This may explain in part why the river's environment is so attractive.

Although roads parallel the river on both sides, population centers are small, spread out, and hardly visible from a canoe. The river teems with wildlife. On one trip in August with the Ka-Na-Wa-Ke Canoe Club of central New York, while we were lunching we saw more than a dozen large blue herons and smaller green herons, a half-dozen mallard ducks, four great horned owls, several red-tailed hawks, and innumerable kingfishers and killdeer, not to mention goldfinches, downy woodpeckers, and even a hummingbird.

The Trip
Start/West Edmeston off NY 8

The river has a low gradient which rarely exceeds a 3- or 4-foot drop over a 20-mile distance. This makes it ideal for the novice paddler; the most that you will encounter at the bends are gentle eddies. Once you've pushed off at West Edmeston you'll find the first mile of the river running a fairly straight course, flowing through a flat valley just a bit over a half mile wide. The forested hills rising on the east are slightly higher and steeper than those on the west. The setting is a most appealing one in which to begin your canoe trip.

Just beyond the mile mark the river starts making a lazy turn to the right, followed by a series of sharper bends to the right and left, until you are on the west side of the valley and just about 200 feet from NY 8. It briefly wanders away from NY 8, then returns, and runs parallel to the highway for about a half mile.

After this brief contact with civilization the river swings again to the east, retreating to a more remote, wooded setting. For the next mile the river's course is straight, and paddling is leisurely. You now pass under a bridge and begin a series of turns which become progressively sharper as you head downstream, covering 1¼ miles before meeting Beaver Creek flowing in from the right.

During the next mile below Beaver Creek the Unadilla begins to shake out its bends; the loops become fewer until they disappear entirely, giving you a long 2¼-mile course which is remarkably straight and pleasingly scenic.

Then you see that the river has finally decided to vary its course, bending first to the left and then to the right. Now there are houses ahead, and a couple more turns bring you to a bridge. The hamlet of South Edmeston lies to the east. You have now come 7.8 miles, just a bit over halfway.

For the next 5¼ miles below South Edmeston, the setting is again rural, with banks heavily tree-lined while forested hills rise on both the left and right, topping out at nearly 1,800 feet. Not a building nor human habitation is to be seen along this stretch, a near-perfect environment for a scenic and leisurely canoe cruise.

A mile below South Edmeston, the Unadilla starts a series of wiggles, twisting back and forth with moderately sharp bends for almost a mile; then it runs a relatively straight course due south for the next 3½ miles to a place where the river narrows considerably and swings to the east, touching the edge of a hillside that rises abruptly upward from the river's edge.

End/Parking area at New Berlin

In little less than a mile more downstream, you begin to see the hills receding on the left, giving way to a broad valley through which flows Wharton Creek. Houses begin to appear on the right, indicating you are approaching New Berlin. A slow turn to the right allows you to see the NY 80 bridge, and below the bridge you can see your parked vehicle and the spot to beach your canoe.

Alternate Canoe Routes

The 62-mile-long Unadilla, with its many access points along NY 8, allows you to plan canoe trips of any length. This is the kind of river that invites you to try a weekend with an overnight stopover en route. You can either tent out or find a motel at a place such as New Berlin.

Since the Unadilla flows into the Susquehanna River at Sidney, you have here a canoe route that can take you into Pennsylvania (see Trip 1). The Susquehanna is moderately broad and deep below Sidney, and you can find take-out points at Bainbridge, Afton, Nineveh, Belden, and even Binghamton.

4

Chenango River

Described Trip:
Sherburne to Norwich
11½ miles
Novice at medium water

Access Points	Interval Distance	Drop and (Gradient)	Trip Time	Water Conditions	Obstacles
Eaton					
	8¼ miles	100' (12)	4 hours	Fastwater, riffles	None
Earlville					
	5½	35' (5)	2	Flatwater	None
Sherburne					
	4½	*32' (7)*	*1½*	*Flatwater*	*None*
North Norwich					
	7	*17' (3)*	*2½*	*Flatwater*	*None*
Norwich					
	9½	55' (6)	3½	Flatwater	None
Oxford					
	36	30' (2)	12	Flatwater	None
Greene					
	24	82' (3)	7½	Flatwater	None
Jct. Susquehanna R. at Binghamton					

USGS (7.5') Maps: Morrisville, Hamilton, Earlville, Norwich, *Oxford, Tyner, Brisben, Greene, Chenango Forks, Castle Creek, Binghamton West.*

The Chenango, like any sensible river, wants to get where it is going without a lot of doodling, but it doesn't want to break any speed records. It sets itself a fairly straight course with bends and oxbows kept to a minimum, but its speed is always moderate—just fast enough so that paddling is easy, and slow enough to let you enjoy your surroundings.

That makes the Chenango ideal water for the novice or family canoeist seeking a relaxing float trip on a sunny day in late spring or early summer, when the landscape is a vibrant green and the river clear and cool.

The Chenango belongs to the Susquehanna Watershed—the central New York south flow—and as such it finds a route through the Chenango Valley in the rolling hill country between the Unadilla River (see Trip 3) in the east, and the Tioughnioga River (see Trip 6) in the west.

In some respects the Chenango resembles both its neighbors. Like the Unadilla, it is a clean, gently flowing river without rapids or chutes. In general, on both the Chenango and the Tioughnioga, the farther downriver you go, the narrower the valley and the steeper the hills become, creating a rugged and handsome landscape.

Still, the Chenango has its own personality which attracts the canoeist. It is one of the longer rivers in the south flow, running 119 miles from its source about two miles north of Morrisville to its junction with the Susquehanna River near Binghamton. Of this length, 72 miles are canoeable.

The Chenango's world is largely a rural one, with only a few urban areas, such as Norwich, found along its route; but even at Norwich one sees parks and recreational areas along the river rather than riverfront buildings or factories. While numerous bridges cross the river, human habitation lies some distance away, permitting the Chenango to preserve its natural appeal.

With its banks grass-covered and tree-lined, the river flows through scenic meadows and farmland typical of the prosperous Chenango Valley. Farther back are forested hills. It is a setting made for canoeing.

If you are so inclined, the easy-going Chenango allows you to mix canoeing with fishing. In its upper reaches (north of Earlville) you'll find fat but spry brown trout or even brook trout in the river's feeder streams, such as Mad Brook just south of Sherburne. Farther downstream are found the warmer water game fish—bass (both large-and smallmouth), northern pike, pickerel, walleye, yellow perch, crappie, and rock bass. In early spring the river is moving slowly enough to let you drift, so you can spincast, flyfish, or even troll from your canoe.

For those who like birding, the river provides an ideal habitat for just about all species found in upstate New York.

Access The Chenango flows south along a line about halfway between Syracuse and Utica. You cross its headwaters on US 20 as you drive into Morrisville from the west.

To get to the access spots, continue east from Morrisville on US 20 until you intersect NY 46. Take NY 46 through Hamilton, following the river on its east side until you reach Sherburne.

Now turn onto US 12 which parallels the river all the way to the village of

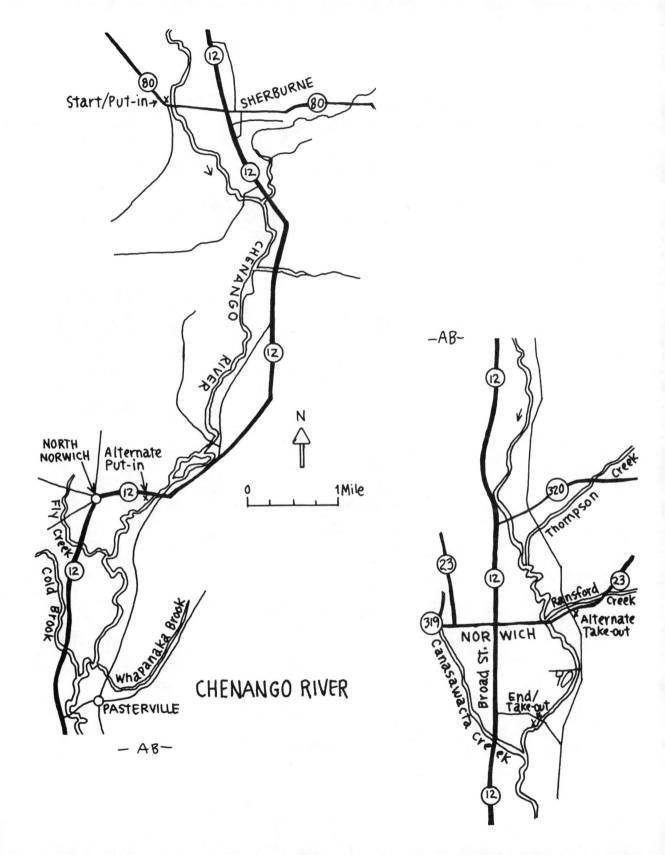

Start/Put-in →

80

12

SHERBURNE

80

CHENANGO RIVER

12

12

N

0   1 Mile

NORTH
NORWICH

Alternate
Put-in

12

Fly Creek

12

Cold Brook

Whapanaka Brook

PASTERVILLE

CHENANGO RIVER

— AB —

— AB —

12

320

Thompson Creek

23

12

319

23

Ransford Creek

Alternate
Take-out

NORWICH

Broad St.

Canasawacta Creek

End/
Take-out

12

Canoeists paddling downstream on the Chenango.

Chenango Forks, running briefly along the river's east side before switching to the west at North Norwich.

You will find a good take-out point just south of Norwich. Drive south on Broad Street from the center of Norwich for six blocks. Turn left, and drive four blocks toward the river. Just before you cross the bridge you'll spot a parking area on your right.

Your put-in point is .5 mile west of the town of Sherburne. Take NY 80 west of Sherburne until it crosses the Chenango. Immediately to your right is state land and an access road to the river. The road is closed to vehicular traffic, but you can easily carry your canoe down this short route. Park your car on the east side of the bridge.

The River
The Chenango is bottom-gazing clear from its source to Norwich. There the river widens and deepens, and also gets a bit murky. By ordinary standards it is a clean river. In its upper sections you'll find little evidence of washed-out trees, and even less of human pollution such as beer cans and picnic trash.

The river makes its way south through the portion of the Appalachian Highlands called the Susquehanna Hills. It begins in Morrisville Swamp, just north of Morrisville, and passes through Eaton, Randellsville, and Earlville en route to Sherburne, a frequently used access point. This portion is usually considered the upper section. Much of it is canoeable in spring and early summer. The middle section runs from Sherburne to Oxford, and the lower from Oxford to the river's junction with the Susquehanna River at Binghamton.

The pitch of the river is gentle; in its 119-mile length it only drops 438 feet, giving it a gradient of 4. This low gradient is why in the mid-1800's the river's valley was selected for one of the Erie Canal feeder systems, the now-abandoned Chenango Canal. The route of this old canal parallels the river on the western side. Sometimes you can see evidence of the canal bed from the river; at other times historic markers indicate the canal's site.

In the river's upper section the valley is wide and the hills low. In the middle section the Chenango Valley narrows considerably and the sides of nearby hills become steep, some even cliff-like. In the lower section the valley widens just slightly, while the hills remain steep.

The Trip
Start/NY 80 bridge
As you put in on the northwest side of the bridge, you'll notice that the river is flowing through a narrow, flat valley about a mile wide. As you paddle downstream the valley starts to narrow and the hills begin to close in. Here the river is fairly wide and shallow. About ½ mile downstream you see two peaked hills across the river on the east—Hunts Mountain to the north, and Sugarloaf Mountain to the south, both with elevations of 1,660 feet.

The river passes under a bridge and swings to the right, hugging the steep-sided and forest-covered Seam Sawmill Hill, which forms the river's western boundary for the next 3½ miles. The canoeist who takes time to climb ashore and search along the river's western bank will find evidence here of the old Chenango Canal.

While the river is tree-lined, much of the lowland near the river is open fields, but soon the trees thicken on your right. At the 3½ mile mark the river splits, forming a small island, and 2 miles below this point it splits again, this time forming a much larger island. The river comes back together just before it passes under the US 12 bridge, ½ mile east of North Norwich. South of this bridge is another good put-in point.

For the next 3½ miles, from the US 12 bridge to the Pasterville bridge, the river meanders about, looping to the left and right, with each bend getting a bit tighter as you progress downriver. It splits briefly just before you reach the Pasterville bridge, and does so again immediately below the bridge.

End/
Third Norwich
bridge

Having got that out of its system, the Chenango begins now to straighten its course; you can see the river well ahead. Along this stretch you have little sense of human habitation. Two-and-a-half miles below the Pasterville bridge you pass under the Woods Corner bridge. From here to the first Norwich bridge the Chenango again presents the paddler with a series of S-turns, adding a little variety to the trip. The city of Norwich sits well off to the right; close to the river are green fields. Soon you pass the second Norwich bridge and a fairground area on the right, and another ¾ mile brings you to the third bridge and your take-out point.

Alternate
Canoe Routes

The Chenango is most accommodating to people planning canoe trips. Access spots such as those in this section's introductory table are numerous, and are found along the river's entire length. In spring and early summer the upper half starting at Earlville gives the best runs. In late summer it might be best to select a route in the lower half, starting at, say, Oxford.

Since the Chenango is well drained and well fed by many tributaries, its water level in the upper reaches is quite respectable. Only in late summer will you start running into riffles and bottomscraping stretches, but all you need to do then is to put in farther downriver, below Norwich.

Because of its length the Chenango is also a good river for weekend or longer trips. Four days is a good period if you want to cruise its entire canoeable length, but a number of shorter options suggest themselves in the middle and lower sections.

5

Otselic River

Described Trip:
Willet to Upper Lisle
7 miles
Novice at medium water
Intermediate at medium high water

Access Points	Interval Distance	Drop and (Gradient)	Trip Time	Water Conditions	Obstacles
South Otselic					
	4 miles	58' (14)	1 hour	Racy runs	None
North Pitcher					
	4.2	21' (5)	1	Flatwater	None
Pitcher					
	4.5	40' (8)	1¼	Flatwater, quickwater	None
Cincinnatus					
	5	43' (8)	1½	Quick	Tree, strainers
Willet					
	9	*35' (4)*	*7*	*Racy, riffles and runs*	*None*
Upper Lisle					
	6	17' (3)	3	Flatwater	None
Whitney Point Dam Spillway					

USGS (7.5') Maps: Otselic, South Otselic, Pitcher, Cincinnatus, Willet, *Whitney Point.*

You can tell when spring arrives in the Otselic valley, not only by the warming weather, but by what appears on or in the water of the Otselic River. Early in April the first fly hatch (*Stenonema Vicarium,* popularly known among fly fishermen as the March Brown) can be seen coming off the water. Two other water-attracted species also appear: the ardent fisherman and the avid canoeist.

For the Indians, "Otselic" referred to the wild plums growing along the river. "Obliging" might better describe this waterway, because the river has arranged things so that the fishermen—spin-casters and fly-casters in their waders and hip boots—are primarily scattered along the upper half of the Otselic, while paddlers occupy the lower half.

For fishing, the Otselic is considered among the top brown trout streams in the state. For canoeing, it is a great river, one of central New York's best to run in spring and early summer. Local paddlers who like their stream between lively and quick make the Otselic their first choice in spring.

This river is always scenic, especially so in spring, when the trees show their first signs of leafing and the river banks their early green shoots. Besides brown trout, the Otselic is the home of osprey and beaver. A good-sized colony of beaver are found about three miles south of your put-in point. You can see their slides and tree cuttings along the river banks in spring.

Access

Put-in and take-out points are easy to find along the Otselic. NY 26 parallels the river, running its entire length, and there are numerous villages and hamlets in the upper half of the Otselic where bridges can be found. In the lower half there are fewer bridges.

An excellent take-out point is found just west of Upper Lisle at the state park called Whitney Point Multiple Use Area, where you can also picnic and camp. In the center of Upper Lisle turn west on Hemlock Road for a short distance to a bridge crossing the Otselic at the upper end of an impoundment. This impoundment is produced by the flood-control dam at Whitney Point, five miles to the south. A boat launching site is next to the bridge on its south side, and nearby are picnic areas and restrooms.

Our put-in point for canoeing the lower section is a spot just west of Willet on NY 41. A new bridge carries NY 41 across the Otselic. On the south side of this road, almost parallel to it and running west from Willet, is the old road that now comes to a dead end at the river. Drive down this road and unload your canoe at the river's edge.

The River

Flanked on the east by the Chenango River (see Trip 10) and on the west by the Tioughnioga (see Trip 12), the Otselic is a tributary of the latter river, and so it is a part of the south flow and the Susquehanna watershed. Its length is 47 miles, of which 38 miles are canoeable.

At medium high water the river's rating is Grade II (medium), and it can be paddled by people who have intermediate (Class III) skill. When, shortly after the spring runoff, the water lowers and the river becomes Grade I (easy), it can be negotiated without difficulty by people in the novice class.

The source of the Otselic is small, privately owned, Torpy's Pond, just north of Georgetown Station. From here the water flows past the communities of

Georgetown, Otselic, South Otselic, North Pitcher, Cincinnatus, Lower Cincinnatus, Willet, and Upper Lisle. At Upper Lisle, when the dam at Whitney Point is closed, the water enters a five-mile-long impoundment—an attractive lake which is excellent for canoe sailing in summer. When the dam is open, as it sometimes is in late spring, you can paddle downstream to the dam itself.

The Trip
Start/
Dead end road
at Willet

At your put-in spot the Otselic is flat and slow, but a scant 100 yards downstream the velocity picks up as the river narrows, to produce a short but sporty run through a set of small standing waves. This is the first of many such runs to be encountered en route; most of them are clear and open passages with moderately swift current.

For the next 1½ miles the river moves moderately, allowing you to take in the surrounding wooded hills and rural valley landscape. Apparently indecisive about which way to go, the Otselic makes an elbow turn to the east, then heads

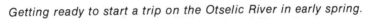

Getting ready to start a trip on the Otselic River in early spring.

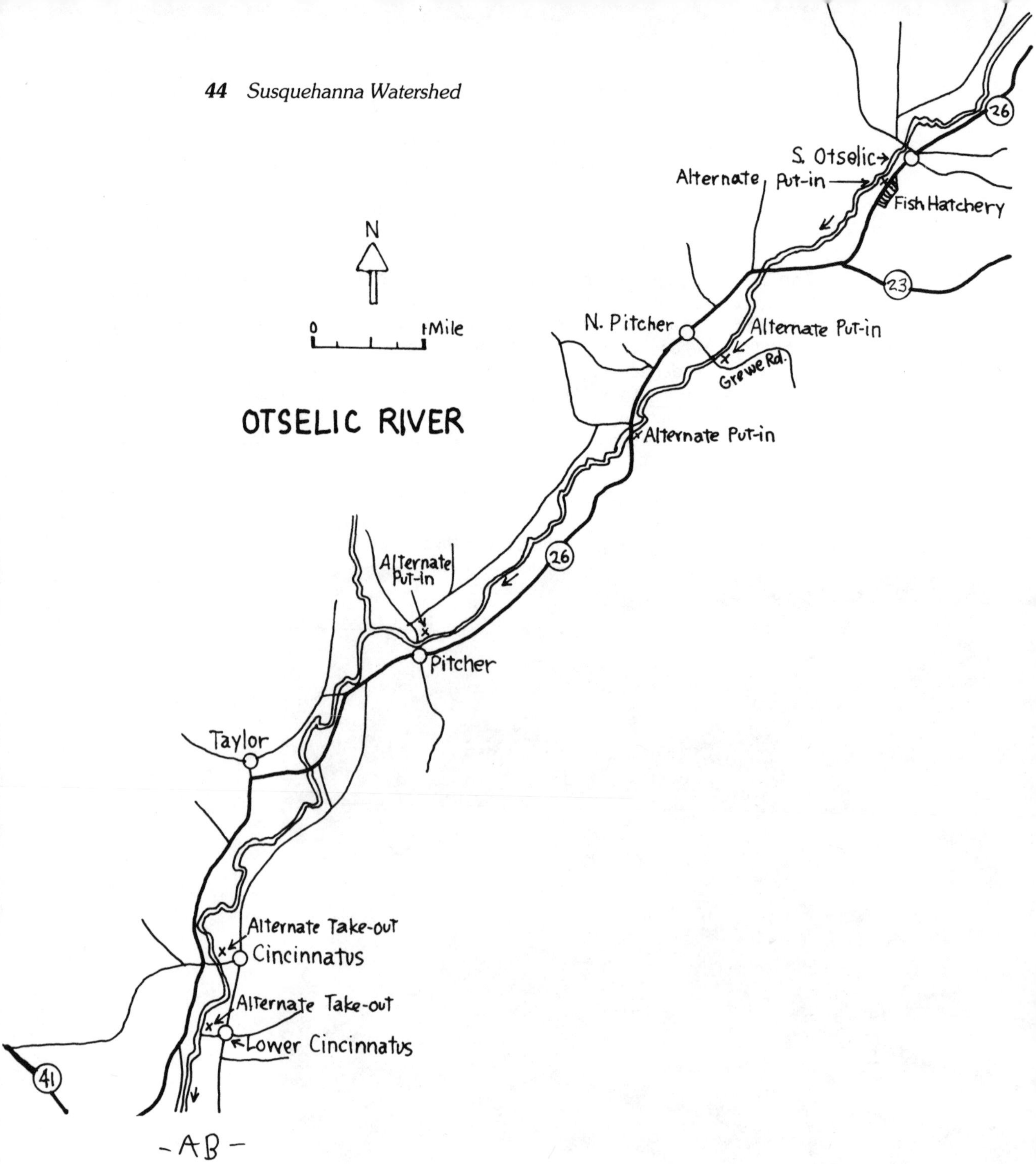

N

0 _____ 1 Mile

OTSELIC RIVER

S. Otselic →

Alternate Put-in →

Fish Hatchery

26

23

N. Pitcher

Alternate Put-in

Grewe Rd.

Alternate Put-in

Alternate Put-in

26

Pitcher

Taylor

Alternate Take-out
Cincinnatus

Alternate Take-out
Lower Cincinnatus

41

– AB –

-A.B-

(41)

(41)
(26)

Willet
(41)

x←
Start / Put-in

(221)

(26)

Merrill Creek

Hemlock Rd.

End/Take-out→
Upper Lisle

Whitney Pt.
Multiple
Use Area

←Whitney Pt. Dam 3.2 Miles

south for a short stretch, then loops west, only to change direction once again by switching back on itself, almost forming an oxbow.

Finally having got its bearings, the Otselic heads briskly southward, picking up speed to provide several nice runs. Soon, 3½ miles from your put-in point, you come to a fairly wide, slow-moving, pond-like section of water where the river swings gently westward. This is not quite halfway but it is a nice place to stop for lunch or a snack break, since it is easy to beach a canoe here and the setting is attractive.

Back in the water, you proceed west around the base of an evergreen-covered hill that provides an almost wilderness setting. Then the river begins a straight, mile-long run south before it loops slowly, first westward, and then south again, to pass under the first road bridge—and the last until you reach Upper Lisle.

In this stretch you encounter several fast but easy runs. You also see signs of beaver on both sides of the river; on the right are beaver slides leading down to the water's edge, and on the left are young saplings that have been cut. This is also the place to look for ospreys, and in spring you can expect to push out ducks that have been resting downstream in slow water.

South of the bridge is a mile of straight river, with the water moving moderately fast. Then the river begins to broaden and slow. The setting also changes: the valleys widen, the trees thin out, and a flat, field-like landscape appears.

End/
Hemlock Road
bridge at
Upper Lisle

The Otselic now picks up the water of Merrill Creek flowing in from the northwest. Ahead the river widens into a large pool as it meets some high ground that rises 30 feet above the river. This bluff falls behind, and after a few slow bends you see on your right evidence of Whitney Point Multiple Use Area, indicating you are approaching your take-out point. Another 1,000 feet downstream brings you to the Hemlock Road bridge. In spring the current here runs fairly swiftly, so paddle downstream and loop back to take out at the boat launching site on the south side of the bridge.

Alternate
Canoe Routes

In the spring when the water is high virtually the entire river is canoeable. Unhappily, much of the land in the upper reaches is posted and, hence, the river is effectively closed to canoeists above South Otselic. Canoeing this section is not recommended.

From South Otselic to Lower Cincinnatus is 13½ miles, a good day's trip. A put-in spot can be found at the fishing access parking area .25 mile south of South Otselic and located on the west side of NY 26 across from the state fish hatchery. You can take out either at the bridge in Cincinnatus or at a spot almost a mile downriver at Lower Cincinnatus, where a bridge crosses the stream. This trip can be shortened by 4 miles if you put in at North Pitcher, or by 8 miles if you put in at Pitcher.

6

Tioughnioga River

Described Trip:
Cortland to Marathon
15 miles
Intermediate at medium water
Novice at low water

Access Points	Interval Distance	Drop and (Gradient)	Trip Time	Water Conditions	Obstacles
Cuyler					
	6 miles	40' (7)	2 hours	Fastwater, riffles	None
Truxton					
	8	25' (3)	2½	Flatwater, riffles	None
East Homer					
	4	35' (9)	1¼	Flatwater	None
Cortland					
	4	20' (5)	1½	Flatwater	None
Blodgett Mills					
	7	50' (9)	2	Flatwater, Fastwater	None
Messengerville					
	4	10' (4)	1½	Flatwater	None
Marathon					
	10	63' (7)	3¼	Flatwater	None
Whitney Point					
	10	65' (7)	3¼		
Chenango Forks					

USGS (7.5') Maps: Otisco Valley, Homer, Cuyler, Cortland, McGraw, Marathon, Lisle, Whitney Point, Green, Chenango Forks.

For its name we can thank the Iroquois Indians. For the river itself and its beautiful setting we are indebted to the late Pleistocene glacier. As this Laurentide ice sheet advanced southward 12,000 years ago across what is now New York State, it rounded off hilltops and deepened valleys, including a narrow north-south cleft cutting through the high uplands that we call the Susquehanna Hills.

The cleft runs from what is today the city of Cortland south to Binghamton, and is the route now taken by the waters of the Tioughnioga River. But long ago, as the glacier retreated, this narrow valley was a drainage system for glacier meltwaters. Torrents of water flooded the valley to Cortland and from there rushed southward through the long cleft, cutting it still deeper to produce a gorge-like trough as the water fed into the Susquehanna River system.

This activity left the canoeist a most attractive legacy. Of all the south-flowing rivers in central New York, the Tioughnioga has the narrowest valleys flanked by the steepest hills. It provides an almost wilderness environment, particularly in the river's middle and lower sections.

After the early spring runoff and flooding subside, the Tioughnioga for the most part becomes a gentle river—ideal for a day's float and for the novice paddler. However, because there are several chutes and runs in the middle section that require fastwater paddling skills, the river has been placed in the intermediate class at medium water.

To the Indians, Tioughnioga meant "Flowers Above the Water." It is possible that the Indians were referring to flowers along the riverbank, because in early summer the banks are festooned with long patches of lavender phlox. On a sunny day this sight can easily turn a canoe trip into a festive occasion.

Access

The headwaters of the Tioughnioga are found just south of Syracuse and north of Cortland. The branches as well as the main stem can be reached easily via US 11, or its close neighbor, I-81. In the river's upper reaches, NY 13 is the highway that follows the East Branch to Cortland; at the southern end, NY 79 follows the river from Whitney Point to Chenango Forks.

You'll have no trouble finding access spots. They exist at virtually every bridge, and there are many bridges crossing the river along its entire length.

The described canoe route is confined to the Tioughnioga's middle section. It is a popular one running from Cortland to Marathon—about a 15-mile float trip. It makes a nice day's cruise with time out for lunch. The trip time (including lunch) is about 5 hours.

The best take-out point is a spot just north of the village of Marathon where the river swings west and touches US 11. Here you will find a large parking area adjoining the river, making it easy to take out the canoe with only a short carry to your vehicle.

An ideal place to launch your canoe is Cortland's Yaman Park, a city picnicking and swimming facility that butts against the Tioughnioga. Yaman Park is located at the east end of Cortland and can be reached via NY 13 and Kennedy Parkway (which brings you to the park entrance). The park charges an entrance fee.

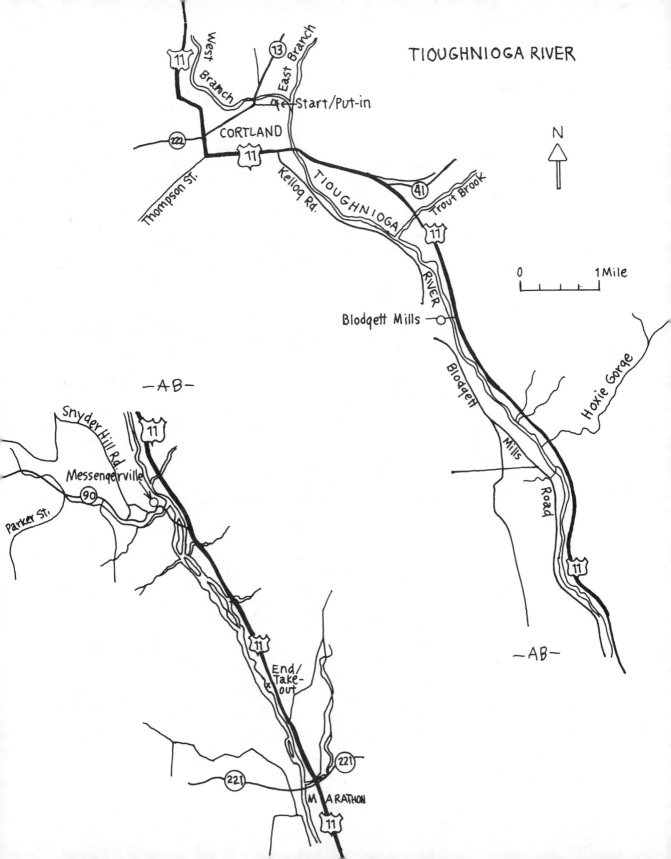

TIOUGHNIOGA RIVER

West Branch

East Branch

Start/Put-in

CORTLAND

Thompson St.

Kellog Rd.

TIOUGHNIOGA

RIVER

Trout Brook

N

0   1 Mile

Blodgett Mills

Blodgett

Mills

Road

Hoxie Gorge

—AB—

Snyder Hill Rd.

Messengelville

Parker St.

End/Take-out

—AB—

MARATHON

The River The Tioughnioga can best be characterized as a straight-running, no-nonsense river that isn't interested in meandering about. If you look on the map you'll see that there are no wiggles, S-turns, or oxbows. Canoeists hardly notice the river's few bends.

However, there is one challenging exception. South of Messengerville bridge the river makes a 90-degree elbow turn to the left, runs a short chute, and does a 90-degree turn to the right. The first turn is manageable; the second is a real thriller calling for fast maneuvering with a right bow rudder and high brace to avoid becoming entrapped in downed tree limbs and the far bank at the bottom of the chute.

The Tioughnioga is an only moderately long river, about 67 miles in length, of which 53 miles are canoeable. Its drop in the canoeable sections is also moderate. From Cuyler (elevation 1,196 feet) to Chenango Forks (elevation 880 feet) the distance is 53 miles, with a 316-foot drop and a corresponding gradient of only 6.

In its upper section the river has two branches. The East Branch begins several miles east of the hamlet of Sheds in the Tioughnioga State Forest (elevation 1,900). The West Branch starts in Green Lake (elevation 1,200), one of a cluster of glacier-created "kettle lakes" that make up what are called the Tully Lakes, all of which are attractive and canoeable (and sailable). These waters flow southward into another set of adjoining lakes at Little York, and then through Homer and Cortland to join the East Branch.

The Trip
Start/
Yaman Park
on NY 13

The Yaman Park launch site allows you to put in where the current is relatively slow. Once in the river you quickly pass under the high I-81 bridge and into a section where the river widens considerably. On days when the water is low you may even scrape bottom in some of the riffle portions.

Buildings on the right quickly give way to more rural scenery which, in turn, changes into a rugged, hilly environment. On the left is US 11, and, if you look closely, on the right you'll see Conrail tracks.

By now the valley has narrowed and the hills have become taller and steeper; the river, correspondingly, has also narrowed and deepened, with the water moving more swiftly. About three miles from your put-in point a small stream, Trout Brook, feeds in from the left, and a mile below the brook you paddle under your first bridge. This one leads to the hamlet of Blodgett Mills.

Below the bridge the landscape becomes more interesting. The river is now running through a valley that is only 800 feet wide; the tree-bedecked hills are steep and impressively high, giving a nice impression of wilderness canoeing. Here and there you encounter riffles, but on the whole the water runs well and moderately deep (a foot or two) for good paddling.

Three miles south of the bridge puts you in the gorge part of the river's middle section. If you have a sharp eye you'll see a small brook on your left. Its source is on top of Hoxie Gorge State Forest on your left, from which the water races downhill through a remarkably deep cut (Hoxie Gorge) and into the Tioughnioga. On your right is more state land, Tuller Hill State Forest (with Tuller Hill itself topping out at 2,000 feet).

You now pass under your second bridge, over which passes NY 90 going

Relaxing on the river.

west to Messengerville and then to Virgil (site of the Greek Peak ski center). The riffles are changing to runs with small standing waves.

Now you come to the sharp S-turn described above. Here the river narrows and the current increases measurably. If you are with a group and have to wait your turn you'll have to put some muscle into your backpaddling to hold your place. The turn here is an elbow bend; the chute, while short, is steep, and the eddy at the bottom is tricky. So be alert and fight for the outside of the pool on your right. If you do, you can make the second sharp turn at the bottom. If not, you'll take a dunking.

End/
Marathon
on US 11
For the next couple of miles the Tioughnioga runs straight and deep, requiring little work from the paddlers. The runs have become gentle with hardly any standing waves. A graceful bend to the left allows you to see some buildings ahead, and a few more minutes of easy canoeing brings you to your take-out point.

Alternate
Canoe Routes
The Tioughnioga divides itself geographically and conveniently into three sections. The upper section, 18 miles in length, runs from Cuyler to Cortland. The 15-mile-long middle section goes from Cortland to Marathon, while the lower section of 18 miles continues from Marathon to Chenango Forks (the location of Chenango Valley State Park with its scores of camping sites).

Any of these sections makes a nice, easy day trip, while a combination of any two or all three makes a good overnight or weekend trip. The upper and middle sections are a bit more popular with local paddlers in the spring. As the water level drops in the summertime, paddling is best on the deeper and wider lower section, which allows good canoeing into late fall.

7

Catatonk Creek/Owego Creek

Described Trip:
Candor to Owego
10 miles
Novice at medium water
Intermediate at medium high water

Access Points	Interval Distance	Drop and (Gradient)	Trip Time	Water Conditions	Obstacles
Spencer					
	3½ miles	27' (8)	2 hours	Fast	Barbed wire, debris
NY 96 bridge					
	¾	9' (1)	¼	Fast	None
W. Candor Rd. bridge					
	2	49' (16)	¾	Fast, moderate	None
Gridleyville Crossing bridge					
	2	10' (5)	¾	Moderate	None
First Dam at Candor					
	¾	*10' (10)*	¼	*Fast*	*None*
Second Dam at Candor					
	2	*20' (10)*	¾	*Fast, moderate*	*None*
Hubbardtown					
	3	*30' (10)*	1	*Fast, moderate*	*None*
Dominick Rd. bridge at Catatonk					
	3	*22' (7)*	*1*	*Moderate*	*Barbed wire*
Jct. with Owego Creek					
	1	*8' (8)*	*⅓*	*Moderate*	*None*
First Owego bridge					
	1	*10' (10)*	*⅓*	Moderate	None
Second Owego bridge					
	½	*10' (20)*	¼	Moderate	None
Jct. Susquehanna					

USGS (7.5') Maps: Spencer, Candor, Owego.

The Catatonk is an ideal stream for novice paddlers. It is, to borrow a New England expression, quickwater—a phrase which means fastwater, but which could serve equally well to describe the kind of water that can quicken the heart, even the heart of the most experienced canoeist. While Catatonk Creek, with the exception of a short stretch above the dam at Candor, is fastwater, it doesn't rush and roar; rather, it runs and chortles—the sights and sounds of a happy stream.

To the paddler, the Catatonk is among the most attractive creeks in the lower region of central New York, popularly known as the Southern Tier. Just as pleasant to look at are the forested hills which surround the creek and which remind many canoeists of Massachusetts' Berkshire Mountains.

It seems that early settlers of this region agreed; they even named several of their communities after those mountains. About fifteen miles north of the city of Owego are Berkshire and East Berkshire, located on opposite sides of Owego Creek.

Another nice fact about this part of central New York's south flow is that you can have three waterways for the price of one—the Catatonk, Owego Creek, and, just a short distance down the lower end of the Owego, the Susquehanna River.

You can paddle all three in one day's outing if you start with the Catatonk, the lively one, and canoe it to where it feeds into Owego Creek, just a mile north of the city of Owego. The combination produces a much wider, but moderately flowing, part of the lower Owego. Two miles downstream, the Owego flows into the broad Susquehanna which is on its way to Pennsylvania, sixteen miles away.

Access   NY 96 runs parallel to the Catatonk for its entire length, providing numerous access points in both its upper and lower reaches.

A popular take-out spot is found at the first, or most northerly, bridge in Owego. As you enter that city from the north, turn right at Tolcott Street and drive several blocks west to the bridge. An open area on the northeast side of the bridge will accommodate four cars. An alternate take-out is a mile downstream at the city's second bridge.

The suggested put-in place is near the first dam in Candor. This dam is located on the northern edge of the village where NY 96 crosses the creek; the dam is just north of the bridge. Descend to the water at the southeast side of the bridge and put in at an eddy. The second dam is ¾ mile downstream.

The Creek   One of Tiogo County's principal waterways, the 22-mile Catatonk stays within the county's boundaries. (Tiogo, to the Indians, meant "water between the hills"—not a bad description of this region.) The main portion of the Catatonk starts with Spencer Lake in the county's northwest corner and ends in the county's central region just north of the city of Owego, where it enters Owego Creek.

From Spencer Lake, the Catatonk flows south 2 miles past Spencer and turns east for 8½ miles to the first dam at Candor, where it again turns south, ending 9½ miles downstream at the junction with the Owego. South of Candor the

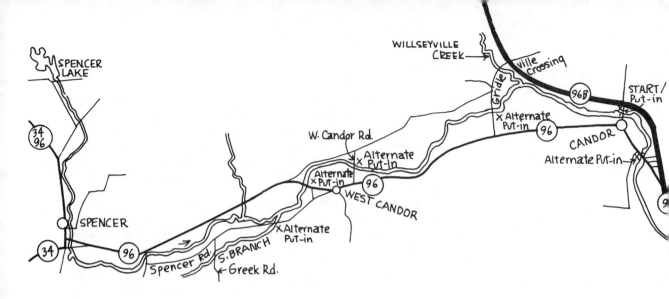

creek flows past the hamlets of Hubbardtown and Catatonk, which are hardly noticeable from the creek.

Catatonk means "rusty water," referring to iron deposits in a spring at the source—not a very apt name, since the water is attractively clear and clean. "Sprightly," might be better, considering the creek's gradient. The Catatonk's drop between Candor and Owego is 190 feet, giving this section a respectable gradient of 19, and explaining why the Catatonk's current is pleasantly lively.

Catatonk's environment is hilly and pastoral. While the hills are not high —only reaching 1,600 feet—they are angular, peaked, and straight-shouldered, which makes them appear taller and more rugged than they really are.

The creek is best canoed from mid-April to mid-May; thereafter the water starts to drop, and you could wind up doing more dragging than paddling.

The Trip
Start/NY 96
Bridge in Candor

If you put in at NY 96 bridge by the first dam in Candor, you'll enjoy a short but sporty run through several glides with small standing waves, to the next dam, ¾ mile downstream. An easy carry around the lower dam puts you back in fastwater for a good stretch downstream. Much of the trip below Candor is made up of runs, with only a few riffles scattered between.

En route you pass over several small drops or "steps" about a foot high. In spring the water is deep enough to permit you to glide or run with ease over these natural stairsteps, rock strata crossing the creek.

The trip to Hubbardtown is straight, with a nice mix of low rapids and runs; there are no twists or turns to slow you down. About 1½ miles south of Hubbardtown, pastureland stretches away from the creek on the left, while tree-covered hills rise on the right. Along here it is easy to put ashore for a lunch break. So pick a nice spot, break out the food, and relax for an hour in this pleasant rural setting.

Back again on the Catatonk, it is a mile to Dominick Road bridge, ½ mile north of the hamlet of Catatonk. In this stretch of water be on the lookout for

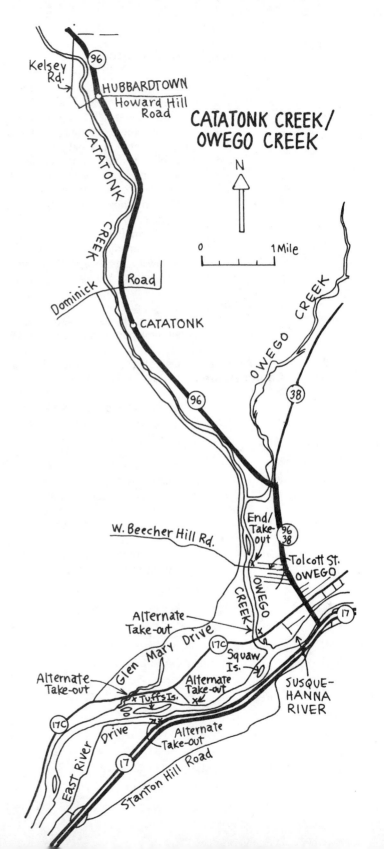

CATATONK CREEK/ OWEGO CREEK

fencing wire crossing the creek. On a trip with the Syracuse-based Ka-Na-Wa-Ke Canoe Club in mid-May, we encountered barbed wire twice along this part of the creek.

Just before reaching Catatonk the creek divides to form an island; stick to the left channel, the better route. A half mile farther downstream you come to another island, a bit larger than the former one; again, stay left. The valley, you will notice, has been narrowing, but as you pass a third island downstream, the hills on the left suddenly fall away and you enter the valley of Owego Creek. Now you know why the Indians called it Owego—"the place where the valley widens."

Just another ½ mile brings you to the Catatonk's junction with Owego Creek. The waterway changes, becoming wider and deeper, and so does its name —now it is the Owego. Downstream ½ mile the Owego splits to produce a fairly long island. Stay in the left channel; it is both faster and deeper.

End/Tolcott Street bridge   Your trip ends as it began—with a nice, fast run through a cluster of small standing waves. Once past the island, the water slows as Tolcott bridge appears ahead. Put ashore at the northeast corner of the bridge. Up a slight embankment is your waiting vehicle.

Alternate Canoe Routes   One alternative is to continue downstream a mile below the Tolcott Street bridge to the Susquehanna River. If you want just a short trip, plan to take out a mile or so beyond your junction with the Susquehanna, around Tuffs Island. Several take-out spots are designated on the map.

If you're after a longer trip, 5½ miles downriver from Tuffs Island is the hamlet of Nichols on the left, with its Kirby Park; another 4 miles brings you to Barton, and 3½ more miles puts you across the border into Pennsylvania en route to Athens, which is 5 miles south of the border, and to Towanda, about 13 miles south of Athens.

In spring when the water level is up, try the upper half of the Catatonk, starting as far upstream as Spencer, but expect to encounter low bridges and barbed wire. A more popular section is the 5-mile run from the NY 96 bridge to Candor, or, putting in a little farther east, the 4-mile stretch from the West Candor bridge to Candor. In spring the water runs well in this section, giving the paddler a fast trip.

Finger Lakes—
Oneida Lake Watershed
(Central Flow)

Fish Creek (West Branch)

Described Trip:
Buell Road bridge to Herder bridge
15½ miles
Upper section: Beginner at medium water
Lower section: Novice at medium water Intermediate at medium high water

Access Points	Interval Distance	Drop and (Gradient)	Trip Time	Water Conditions	Obstacles
Kasoag Lake					
	5 miles	259' (53)	1½ hours	Flatwater	Shallow, brush alders
Williamstown					
	6½	20' (3)	2	Flatwater	Dam
Westdale					
	7	50' (7)	2½	Flatwater, runs, riffles	Dam
Camden					
	5½	30' (6)	2	Flatwater	None
Buell Rd. Bridge					
	5	*20' (4)*	*2*	*Flatwater*	*None*
McConnellsville					
	4½	*40' (9)*	*1½*	*Flatwater Fastwater, runs, riffles*	*Dam*
Jct. East Branch					
	6	*28' (5)*	*2*	*Flatwater Runs, riffles*	*None*
Herder Bridge					
	5½	1' (0)	2	Flatwater	None
Fish Creek Landing					
	2¼	1' (0)	1	Flatwater	None
Jct. Barge Canal					
	1	0' (0)	½	Flatwater	None
Sylvan Beach/Lake Ontario					

USGS (7.5') Maps: Williamstown, Westdale, Camden West, Camden East, Lee Center, Sylvan Beach.

59

Its name may be commonplace, but as a scenic canoeable waterway Fish Creek has few equals. For the paddler, the two upper branches of the Fish are top quality streams, providing some of the best views and finest water in upstate New York.

If you are an angler who has fished this creek, you know that its name wasn't idly bestowed. In its upper branches are large, sassy brown trout; and in the lower end hefty walleyes can be found; with generous sprinklings of other game fish such as bass, pike, and pickerel in both middle and lower sections.

Moving upstream, Fish Creek divides near Blossvale to form a huge "Y," splitting into the East and West Branches. The word "creek" belies the river-like character of the branches' lower portions. In particular, the West Branch is wide and handsome for more than two-thirds of its distance.

A remarkable quality of Fish Creek and its two branches is their total length—91 miles, of which about 60 miles is not only canoeable, but which flows through some of the most attractive landscape in central New York.

The Fish is a creek with three personalities. The East Branch is the lively one; it is fast, even turbulent, in many stretches as it races from the top of Tug Hill through a gorge-like wilderness to meet the West Branch just south of Taberg. The West Branch flows through a flatter, forested terrain, and is more subdued in behavior. The main stem at the lower end is broad and meandering, flowing unhurriedly between high steep banks in flat open country.

The three sections are so different that one can hardly believe they belong together. But this gives the Fish qualities always sought by canoeists: lots of choices in water, terrain, and scenery.

Access   The West Branch is located north of Oneida Lake, hugging the southern slope of Tug Hill. While it begins in Oswego County, it spends most of its time in Oneida County.

The stream's many access points can easily be reached by NY 13 which, in turn, can be reached off I-81 in the north at Pulaski, or off I-90 in the south at Canastota. Coming from the north, NY 13 crosses the West Branch at Williamstown and then follows the stream in its southeasternly journey to McConnellsville.

Your take-out point is the north side of Herder bridge, which can be reached by NY 49 via Rome, 10 miles to the east, or via Central Square, 27 miles to the west. You can also take NY 13 north out of Canastota through Sylvan Beach to its intersection with NY 49 just west of Vienna. Turn right (east) onto NY 49, and 5.8 miles brings you to Herder bridge.

To get to your put-in point at Buell Road bridge, follow NY 49 back to Vienna where it intersects NY 13. Turn north on NY 13 and drive past McConnellsville toward Camden. It is 5.6 miles from Vienna to Buell Road, which intersects on the right. Turn here and drive .8 mile to the bridge crossing the West Branch. Park, and take your canoe down the footpath that can be found on the right side of the road.

If you wish to put in farther upstream, there are several nice access spots at Blakesley Road (immediately north of Buell Road), at Brewer Road, and in Camden. In the spring you can put in as far north as Westdale or Williamstown.

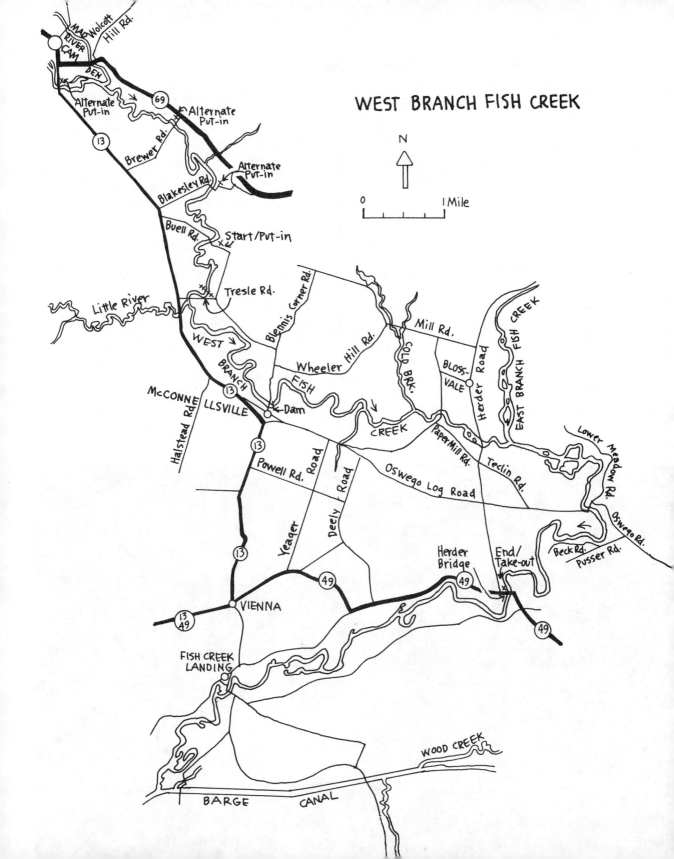

WEST BRANCH FISH CREEK

N

0   1 Mile

Wolcott Hill Rd.

MAD RIVER CAM DEN

69

Alternate Put-in

Alternate Put-in

Alternate Put-in

13

Brewer Rd.

Blakesley Rd.

Buell Rd.

Start/Put-in

Tresle Rd.

Little River

WEST BRANCH

Blennis Corner Rd.

Wheeler Hill Rd.

FISH

Mill Rd.

COLD BRK.

BLOSS-VALE

Herder Road

EAST BRANCH FISH CREEK

McCONNELLSVILLE

13

Halstead Rd.

Dam

13

CREEK

Paper Mill Rd.

Teclin Rd.

Lower Meadow Rd.

Powell Rd.

Road

Deely Road

Oswego Log Road

Oswego Rd.

Beck Rd.

Pusser Rd.

Yeager

49

Herder Bridge

End/Take-out

49

49

13 49

Vienna

FISH CREEK LANDING

WOOD CREEK

BARGE   CANAL

The Creek The West Branch begins at an elevation of 819 feet in a cluster of ponds which are collectively identified as Kasoag Lake. From here to West's junction with the East Branch the drop is 419 feet for a gradient of 12. In contrast, the East Branch, with its source on the very top of Tug Hill (elevation 2,008), drops 1,608 feet before it reaches its junction with the West Branch, for an impressive gradient of 37.

That gives you a clue to the difference between the two branches. The West Branch is in no rush to get to Lake Oneida; this is most noticeable from Buell Road bridge to the dam at McConnellsville, where the drop is only 20 feet, for a gradient of 4. The West Branch is ideal for novice and family canoeists.

The McConnellsville dam also helps the upper part of the West Branch to hold its water well into summer. The section from Camden to McConnellsville is canoeable without scraping bottom in late summer, while the section below the dam may display a number of bottom-scraping stretches at that time.

Although Fish Creek and its two branches are south-flowing streams, their water flows into Lake Oneida, which, in turn, empties into Lake Ontario via Oneida River and Oswego River. This makes Fish Creek part of the St. Lawrence watershed.

While civilization is never far away from the West Branch, the hilly terrain in and near the stream is forested. From Buell Road bridge to Herder bridge you rarely see a house. Instead, you have a sense of remoteness, even of a wilderness setting, as you float downstream.

Soloing on lower section of Fish Creek.

The Trip
Start/Buell Road bridge

At the put-in point, the water flows deep and gentle through a heavily wooded area. Soon the stream begins a series of twists and turns, looping back on itself several times for about ½ mile before straightening out.

A half mile of straight water takes you under a railroad bridge before swinging to the right past a high bank on the left. The water picks up speed to give you a nice run for the next 100 yards. Then it deepens again.

The next sharp turn to the left brings you under a road bridge and into a heavily forested section with large stands of evergreens. On the right just past the bridge is a small feeder stream, Little River.

The West wanders southeastward in a series of long, lazy loops that takes you first to the left side of the valley and then to the right. In this 3-mile stretch the stream begins a deepening that continues as you approach the dam at McConnellsville, home of a sizeable furniture factory.

You take out on your left immediately after passing under the bridge, and carry around the dam on the lefthand side. The water below the dam is broad and shallow, but it soon narrows and grows deeper as you head downstream.

In this section the water moves much faster than it did above the dam. The scenery for the next 3½ miles is similar to that found upstream—forested, but with fewer evergreens. The landscape has become more hilly, with tree-covered banks rising as high as 40 feet.

The turns are less pronounced, now, and you encounter several small river islands. As the water's velocity increases you also encounter riffles and runs. In spring, when the water level is higher, there are small rapids with foot-high standing waves.

Shortly after the woods on the left give way to fields, you pass under your first bridge since McConnellsville. Woods continue on the right. In the next mile you pass under a second road bridge, and then you meet the East Branch coming in on the left. Fish Creek now widens considerably. A half mile downstream the water splits three ways, producing two sizeable islands with the main channel running between them.

End/Herder Bridge

The banks have become higher, straighter, and increasingly devoid of trees. Fish Creek now turns south, and after several slow loops, turns back on itself heading west, but within a mile it again turns south. You now become aware of many holes drilled into the sides of the tall, cliff-like banks on your right —homes of bank swallows that are busy flitting in and out, feeding their young. The creek has a couple more turns left in its system before it gives you a short straight run to Herder bridge.

Alternate Canoe Routes

The West Branch offers a number of route choices, depending on the canoeist's timetable. In spring, or for those who like canoe poling, the upper section from Williamstown to Westdale is a good option. The section upstream from the dam in Westdale is particularly good, with the water deep and slow-moving. Upstream ½ mile from the Westdale dam you can pick up a feeder stream that allows you to paddle into a small pond called Gifford Lake.

On the East Branch in spring and early summer, a good stretch of canoeable water runs 3 miles from Taberg to the junction with the West Branch. Below Herder bridge you have over 8 miles of slowwater for a lazy float downstream.

9

Oneida River/Oneida Lake

Described Trip:
Brewerton to Schroeppel bridge
9½ miles
Novice at medium water

Access Points	Interval Distance	Drop and (Gradient)	Trip Time	Water Conditions	Obstacles
Brewerton					
	3½ miles	4' (1)	1¼ hours	Flat	None
Jct. Caughdenoy Creek					
	½	0' (0)	¼	Flat	Dam, control gates
Caughdenoy					
	3	0' (0)	1	Flat	None
Jct. Anthony Cut					
	1	0' (0)	⅓	Flat	None
Glosky Island					
	1½	0' (0)	½	Flat	None
Schroeppel bridge					
	2	5' (2)	¾	Flat	None
Island Rd. bridge					
	2¼	0' (0)	¾	Flat	None
Three Rivers					

USGS (7.5') Maps: Brewerton, Central Square, *Baldwinsville*

When the long dry summer takes its toll of your favorite streams, reducing them to trickles, the Oneida River—high, wide, and handsome—is a welcome sight. With Oneida Lake feeding in water at the east end, and control gates regulating the water level at Caughdenoy, the Oneida is never short of water, and neither are the lucky canoeists who live nearby.

The water level is maintained because the Oneida River is part of New York's Barge Canal system, but this man-made asset is balanced by a drawback, also man-made. The river is a popular route for large and small power boats, especially on weekends, and wakes from fast boat traffic can make canoeing a rocky experience.

Still, the Oneida is too good a waterway to be surrendered to power boats. If you time your outings intelligently you can avoid most of the problem. Weekdays are good because then traffic is down. Another possibility is to canoe here in the spring before the locks are open, or in the late fall after the locks are closed. At those times the power boats desert the Oneida, and canoeists have the whole river to themselves.

The Oneida River, as well as the Indians after whom the waterway is named, played strategic roles in the early history of this region. As an outlet of Oneida Lake, the largest lake wholly within New York's boundaries, the Oneida River feeds into Oswego River (see Trip 17) and then into Lake Ontario. It was—and still is—the main water route to the Great Lakes and Canada, and it was extensively used by the Iroquois Indians and later by explorers, traders, and missionaries.

Samuel de Champlain discovered Oneida Lake on October 8, 1615. The important Indian village Techiroguen was located at the river's origin at Oneida Lake. Techiroguen was visited by Father Simon LeMoyne in 1654, and by Sieur de La Salle in 1673.

The Onondagas occupied the territory west and south of Oneida Lake, the Oneida nation the east end of the lake. Surprisingly, it was the peaceful Oneidas who did the most to halt the original French colonizing efforts. When Champlain tried to subdue the Oneidas he found them to be fierce defenders of their land. Champlain was wounded and his forces defeated at Nichols Pond near Canastota, forcing him and his troops to retreat to Canada.

Later the British, knowing the military importance of the lake and river, erected Fort Brewerton at the outlet in 1759. Thirty years later the first settler, Oliver Stevens, moved into the Brewerton area, and in 1818 George C. Schroeppel, for whom the town of Schroeppel is named, built the first frame house near today's Schroeppel bridge—our described trip's take-out spot.

Some naturalists think of the Oneida as the river of ducks. Mallards like the upper part of the river, probably because hunting is prohibited on a section of the outlet. In spring through early summer they nest and raise their young here; as you paddle downstream you'll see scores of mallards on the river or flying short distances ahead of your canoe. There are probably more mallards per canoeable mile on the Oneida than on any other stream in central New York.

Access   A half dozen different roads run parallel to the Oneida River at different places, and several of these cross the river, providing easy access.

The suggested take-out spot for this trip is Schroeppel bridge, at about the river's halfway point. The bridge can be reached by Morgan Road, 7.8 miles north from the center of Liverpool village on Onondaga Lake.

The put-in is at Brewerton, on the south side of the river. From Syracuse, take US 11 into Brewerton. Just before you reach the Oneida River bridge, turn left (west) on Bennett Street. Drive one block and turn right on Walnut Street, which immediately brings you to the river's edge. There's room here to park several cars. A low depression in the concrete abutment by the river allows you to launch your canoe easily.

The River   As the crow flies it is only 7¼ miles from the western edge of Oneida Lake to Three Rivers, where the Oneida River joins the Seneca River to form the Oswego River, yet it takes the Oneida 18¼ miles to make that trip. Although the Oneida is not a long river, it does its best to be one, stretching itself out in the lowlands north of Syracuse, and in the process it shows the canoeist a lot of countryside.

When the state's Barge Canal was constructed shortly after 1900, it was decided to shorten the Oneida's water route 8 miles by cutting ditches across the bottom of the river's several loops. The two largest ditches are Anthony Cut and Big Ben Cut; each forms a man-made island. Two other smaller and unnamed cuts produced Glosky Island and Schroeppel Island. As a result, you now have something akin to an aquatic labyrinth.

The control gates are located at Caughdenoy, and at Lock 23 at the west end of Anthony Cut. When the gates are closed in spring the river is high again, and the lock, with its 6.9-foot vertical rise, goes into use. There's not much of a drop in the Oneida from its source at the lake to its terminus at Three Rivers—only about 7 feet, for a low gradient, indeed.

The Oneida has one major feeder stream, Caughdenoy Creek, just ½ mile south of the hamlet of Caughdenoy. Be sure to include it on your itinerary. It is about two canoe lengths wide and several feet deep, with a gentle current that makes upstream paddling easy. The creek is heavily lined with trees, mostly shagbark hickory. Serenity is a word that fits the lower section of this creek up to the first beaver dam, a short distance from Caughdenoy—Central Square road. The creek narrows thereafter, but you can paddle, or, better still, pole your way another 2½ miles to the NY 49 bridge.

The Trip   The Oneida can be said to begin at the US 11 bridge, just above your put-in
Start/Brewerton   spot at the end of Walnut Street in Brewerton. But even here the river is about 600 feet wide, a width it maintains for most of its course. You are hardly aware there is a current. The first couple of miles downstream look relatively civilized, with small frame houses nestled among the trees along both shores.

A little less than 1½ miles downstream you see a straight waterway branching off on your left. This is Anthony Cut, the route of canal traffic. Bear to your right and continue downstream on the Oneida. Houses and trees are gradually replaced by fields and highways, but then a mile downstream the houses and trees return.

When you are about 1½ miles from Anthony Cut, start looking for Caughdenoy Creek on your right. Soon after you spot the creek you pass under the County Route 37 bridge, and paddle past several houses into a quiet,

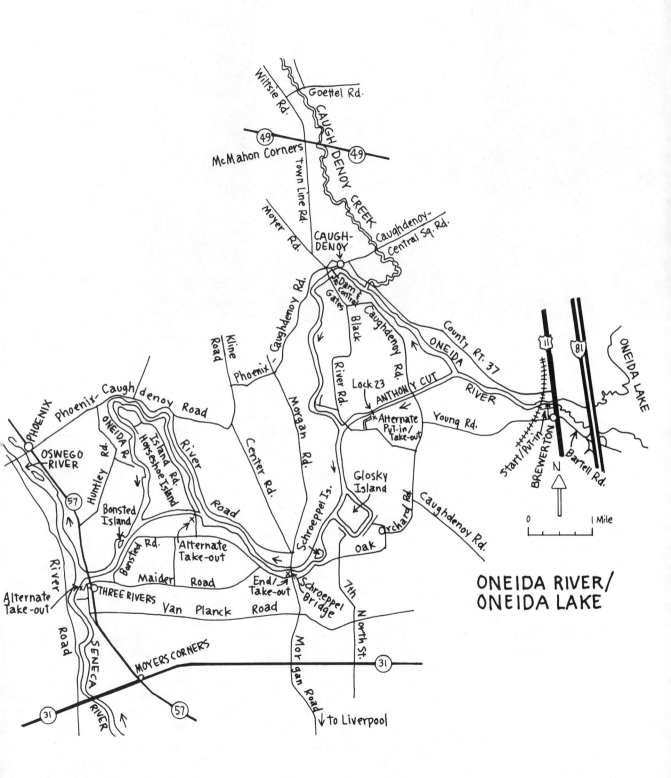

ONEIDA RIVER/
ONEIDA LAKE

Oneida River (on right) and Seneca River (on left) join to form Oswego River at Tree Rivers.

canopied world that seems far removed from civilization. The slow-flowing creek, snaking back and forth, finally brings you to a beaver dam, 1¼ miles upstream. Behind the dam are some dead trees, and just beyond, the Caughdenoy-Central Square road. This beaver dam is a good place to turn around and head down the creek.

Back on the Oneida, it is ½ mile to the river's bend, site of Caughdenoy hamlet and the river's control gates. Take out on the river's right side and carry around the gates. The current on the other side is fairly swift, but it soon slows as the water deepens. You now have a 2½-mile paddle to the spot where the Oneida meets the water flowing through Anthony Cut. Lock 23 is ¼ mile up the cut—a possible take-out, or a place to have lunch.

End/Schroeppel bridge

Trees again have thickened along the shore; a little over a mile downstream you see a waterway cutting off shortly on the left, indicating you have reached Glosky Island. A 1½-mile loop brings you around the tree-covered island, and another ½ mile finds you at Schroeppel bridge and your take-out spot.

Alternate Canoe Routes

The obvious option is the lower section of Oneida from Schroeppel bridge to Three Rivers. You can take the long route of 7 miles around Horseshoe Island, or the shorter 3-mile route through Big Ben Cut. Your take-out is on the west side of NY 57 at a small park-like area where there is ample space for cars.

A shorter but attractive route is the 2-mile long Anthony Cut. From Brewerton to Lock 23 on the Cut is about 3 miles for a short afternoon workout.

The western end of Oneida Lake is ideal for canoe sailing and, if time permits, fishing for bass and walleyes among the weedbeds on the lake's south side.

10

Seneca River (Lower)/Onondaga Lake

Described Trip:
Baldwinsville to Belgium
12½ miles
Novice at medium water

Access Points	Interval Distance	Drop and (Gradient)	Trip Time	Water Conditions	Obstacles
Baldwinsville					
	3 miles	*10' (3)*	*1 hour*	*Flat*	*None*
Red Rock					
	2	*5' (2)*	*¾*	*Flat*	*None*
Klein Island					
	1 ¼	*2' (1)*	*½*	*Flat*	*None*
Long Branch					
	1 ¼	*3' (1)*	*½*	*Flat*	*None*
NY 370 bridge					
	1	*0' (0)*	*⅓*	Flat	None
Elmcrest					
	4	0' (0)	*1½*	*Flat*	*None*
Belgium					
	2	0' (0)	*¾*	Flat	None
Three Rivers					

USGS (7.5') Maps: Baldwinsville, Camillus, Syracuse West, Brewerton

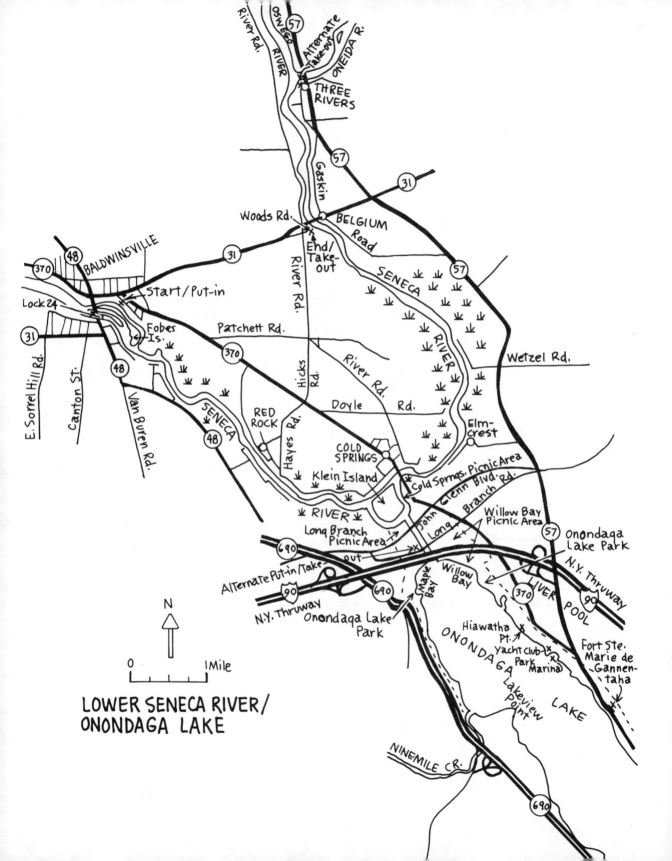

LOWER SENECA RIVER /
ONONDAGA LAKE

Sometimes things are too close at hand to be fully appreciated. This frequently happens with waterways that are just down the road, or that are next to civilization. The appeal of remote and pristine wilderness is absent, and so is our interest in canoeing that water.

This is almost the case with the Seneca River's lower section—the section that starts at Baldwinsville, loops south to touch Onondaga Lake, and then swings north to join Oneida River, forming the Oswego River. Almost, but not quite, since many canoeists from racers to recreational paddlers make good use of this portion of the Seneca throughout the canoeing season. And for several good reasons:

On the Seneca you are never without water. As part of the New York Barge Canal, the Seneca's level is controlled, guaranteeing plenty of water when summer has virtually dried up other nearby streams.

The river is flatwater the whole way, which attracts beginner and novice paddlers, since they can easily canoe upstream or downstream. It is also the kind of water that racing and marathon paddlers use to keep in shape. Expect to see low, sleek canoes propelled by bent paddles on this river; they're the racers.

Another feature is the Seneca's short tie-in with Onondaga Lake, which means that you have access to the large, attractive Onondaga Lake Park arching around the lake's northwestern end. Here you can picnic and relax. More important, you can also put in here to canoe-paddle the river or canoe-sail the lake or, better still, do both. You don't have to use your own canoe, since there is a canoe rental concession in the park at Long Branch Road.

If you're a bird watcher the way to go is by canoe, allowing you to observe the large variety of shore birds that, particularly during migration periods, use the lake's beaches. And if you like a scenic, tree-lined river, the Seneca is happy to oblige; little of the civilization surrounding the Seneca breaks through at the river's edge, which is generally heavily wooded throughout its length.

The Seneca also flows through a region rich in history. This is the land of Hiawatha, who, indeed, was a real person and a great chief, and who stood before the assembled chiefs of all the Iroquois nations on the banks of Onondaga Lake and forged the great Iroquois Confederacy that was to last for 200 years.

This, too, is the home of the Onondagas, "the people of the great hills," whose Long House served as the capital of the Iroquois Confederacy. Here are found the names of three of the five Iroquois nations: Seneca, Oneida, and Onondaga. It was in this region that the first contact was made between Indian and white man—French explorers, traders, and missionaries came in the early 17th century, men like Samuel de Champlain, Sieur de La Salle, Pierre Esprit Radisson (for whom the community of Radisson is named), and Father Simon LeMoyne (for whom LeMoyne College is named).

Father LeMoyne made contact with the Onondagas in 1654; they greeted him warmly, and five days later he met with the chiefs of the Five Nations. Near this meeting place on Onondaga Lake a fort, Ste. Marie de Gannentaha, was built. A replica is found today in Onondaga Lake Park, overlooking the lake.

Access   Your take-out is found at the end of Woods Road on the southwest side of the NY 31 bridge as it crosses into the hamlet of Belgium, 1.8 miles south of Three Rivers. Woods Road angles off NY 31 and runs a short distance to the river's edge, where you'll find room to park several vehicles.

The put-in spot is located behind the Town of Lysander office building, situated almost on the corner of Lock and Genesee Streets in the center of Baldwinsville. There's a large parking lot behind the building, adjacent to the river. You'll be launching your canoe on the north side of the river, a short distance below the falls and the NY 48 bridge. On the river's south side you'll find Lock 24.

**The River
and Lake**   The river has its origin at Seneca Lake, on the east side of Geneva. From here it flows eastward to pick up the outlet water of Cayuga Lake, and then heads in a northeasterly direction to Cross Lake and then to Baldwinsville. The river swings in a southeastern direction around Klein Island, where it merges with the outlet of Onondaga Lake, and then turns north to meet Oneida River at the community of Three Rivers. At this confluence the Oswego River is formed.

This 47-mile route makes the Seneca part of the Finger Lakes-Oneida Lake watershed and, with the addition of Oswego River (see Trip 17), eventually a part of the Lake Ontario-St. Lawrence north flow. As part of the New York Barge Canal, the Seneca is a broad, slow-moving waterway. Commercial traffic moves on the Seneca, but much of the daily traffic is made up of pleasure boats.

The Seneca can be divided conveniently into an upper section that runs from Seneca Lake to Howland Island (see Trip 11), the middle from Howland Island to Cross Lake, and the lower from Cross Lake to Three Rivers. The upper section is the most industrialized and urbanized; the middle the least. The lower, while flowing through a heavily populated region, much of it suburban, shows surprisingly little of this civilization along the river's edge. As a matter of fact, the 5-mile stretch from the NY 370 bridge to Belgium is almost devoid of human habitation.

Syracuse encircles the southern part of Onondaga Lake, while Liverpool runs along its northern shore. Over the years the county has acquired land around the lake's northern and western edges, creating an attractive green belt called Onondaga Lake Park. North of Long Branch Road, the park continues along the lake outlet to the Seneca River as Long Branch Picnic Area on the west, and as Cold Springs Picnic Area on the east.

In the early 1800's, the area around the lake became famous for its many salt springs, which were responsible for Syracuse's early development; later it was the salt wells and the mixture of salt and limestone to form soda ash that were to make Syracuse famous as "Salt City." The city and lake are still famous, but now it is because they are the site of the Intercollegiate Rowing Association's annual two-day regatta, featuring the best four- and eight-man shells in the country.

The Trip
Start/Baldwinsville   Once you've parked behind the town office building, it is a quick and easy carry to the river. The village of Baldwinsville lies behind you, and a short distance upstream is the NY 48 bridge and the Baldwinsville dam. The river is

A take-out spot on the Onondaga Lake Outlet.

fairly wide here, containing several islands, but as you head downstream and round the point of Fobes Island, the river narrows to a normal width.

Houses can be seen on your right, but on your left the river bank is tree-covered all the way to the hamlet of Red Rock, on the north shore 3 miles below your put-in. Houses appear on both sides of the river for the next mile; thereafter they disappear on the right, and then give way to a thickening woods on your left. A mile farther downstream brings you to tree-covered Klein Island, which is 1½ miles in circumference.

Take the right channel and follow it for ¾ mile to the place where it meets the outlet of Onondaga Lake. Turn right now and canoe up the outlet past Syracuse University's crewing headquarters and the two county parks, to the junction with the lake and Willow Bay Picnic Area. You can put ashore here and take a lunch break, using the park's table and picnic facilities.

For those interested in observing shore birds or in merely exploring the lake, try the west shore at Maple Bay. About a 2-mile paddle takes you southward to where you encounter the inflow of Ninemile Creek; here the county park ends.

Returning to Willow Bay, you can continue your trip by paddling back down the outlet to Klein Island. Stay in the right channel and ¾ mile brings you to the NY 370 bridge that crosses north into the hamlet of Cold Springs. From here it is a mile to Elmcrest, a cluster of homes situated on high ground on the right.

End/NY 31 bridge   The woods on both sides of the river now thicken; from here to your take-out at Belgium the river is without noticeable human habitation, just dense vegetation and solid green. Ahead you can see the Belgium bridge over which passes NY 31. Bear to the left, and take out at the southwest side of the bridge.

Alternate Canoe Routes   One option is to put in at the Jordon Road bridge just west of Cross Lake (or at Jacks Reef bridge about 2 miles east of Cross Lake), and paddle eastward for 14½ miles through a rural section made up of small farms and pastureland to Baldwinsville.

Still another possibility is Onondaga Lake itself. There is an access point where Long Branch Road crosses the outlet. On a calm day you can try canoeing around the lake, a distance of 10 miles; or, if there is a good breeze, break out your sails and let the wind take you around the lake.

11

Seneca River (Upper)

Described Trip:
Yellow Schoolhouse Road bridge
around Howland Island
9 miles
Novice at medium water

Access Points	Interval Distance	Drop and (Gradient)	Trip Time	Water Conditions	Obstacles
Boat launch site at Yellow School-house Road bridge					
	1½ miles	0' (0)	1½ hours	Flatwater	None
Mosquito Point bridge					
	1½	0' (0)	1½	Flatwater	None
Hard Point Road					
	7½	0' (0)	4	Flatwater	None
Yellow Schoolhouse Road bridge					

USGS (7.5') Maps: Geneva South, Geneva North, Seneca Falls, Cayuga, Montezuma, Weedsport, Jordon, Lysander, Baldwinsville, Camillus, Brewerton.

One of the three big waterways of central New York, the Seneca is a river that has been tamed and put to work as part of New York's Barge Canal system which runs from Buffalo to Albany. It has been urbanized in many sections, such as the stretch from Geneva to Seneca Falls where communities with their factories sit astride the river. But the canoeist's Seneca is the part of the river that flows through rural areas, meandering past low rolling countryside, and through long wooded sections where you can't spot a house for miles.

A good example of the rural Seneca is the 9-mile loop that runs around the state's Howland Island Wildlife Management Area—an attractive multi-use area dotted with man-made ponds which serve as resting, feeding, and nesting places for native and migratory waterfowl.

While a true island, Howland itself is man-made. Early in this century, when engineers were building the Barge Canal to replace the old Erie Canal, they cut an east-west ditch across the southern part of a horseshoe-like loop in the Seneca, creating Howland Island.

The scenery along this island waterway is mostly wooded, featuring typical riverbottom trees—willow, ash, and red maple. With the exception of a few houses found at the end of Hard Point Road, there are no signs of human habitation around the entire circle.

What you do find in great abundance, however, especially during migratory seasons, is birdlife. Common among the larger species are duck, Canada geese, various hawks, blue and green heron, and turkey vultures (which are extending their range farther to the east). Scores of smaller birds, ranging from shore birds through woodpeckers and flycatchers to warblers and orioles, can be seen near Howland Island. So bring your binoculars.

While you can canoe this route at any season, wait for midsummer, when other choice streams begin drying up. There is no water level problem on the Seneca; it always runs full and deep. Ideal for family canoeing, with trees arching over the water, this part of the river is invariably pleasant and, even on hot summer days, cool. Powerboats do not run here; this section of the river is used almost exclusively by canoeists. You can hardly find a current. So it is a slow, leisurely float with nothing to disturb the quiet except the sound of your blade pushing through water.

Access Because you are circling an island your put-in and take-out points are the same—the island's boat launching site immediately on your right as you cross the island bridge. This is the best spot, but you can also find access farther down the river at the Mosquito Point bridge crossing, or upstream at the end of Hard Point Road.

To reach the boat launching site, take NY 38 north out of Port Byron and drive 2 miles to Yellow Schoolhouse Road which turns left just before the bridge that crosses Owasco Lake Outlet (a good canoeable waterway). Follow Yellow Schoolhouse Road for 1.8 miles to the one-lane steel bridge that crosses the canal to Howland Island. The boat launching site is on the other side of this bridge.

The River As the Seneca Indians were the tallest warriors among the Iroquois (many over six feet), the Seneca River is the longest river of central New York's big three

Canoeing the Seneca River around Howland Island.

—Seneca, Oneida, and Oswego—that make up the central portion of the Barge
Canal system. The river runs 47 miles through a broad valley plain along the
southern edge of the Ontario drumlin region. Howland Island is itself a cluster
of haystack-like drumlins.

The source of the Seneca is Seneca Lake (66.7 square miles) which is the
largest of the Finger Lakes, just a fraction bigger than its kissing cousin,
Cayuga Lake (66.4 square miles). Both Seneca and Cayuga Lakes are 40 miles

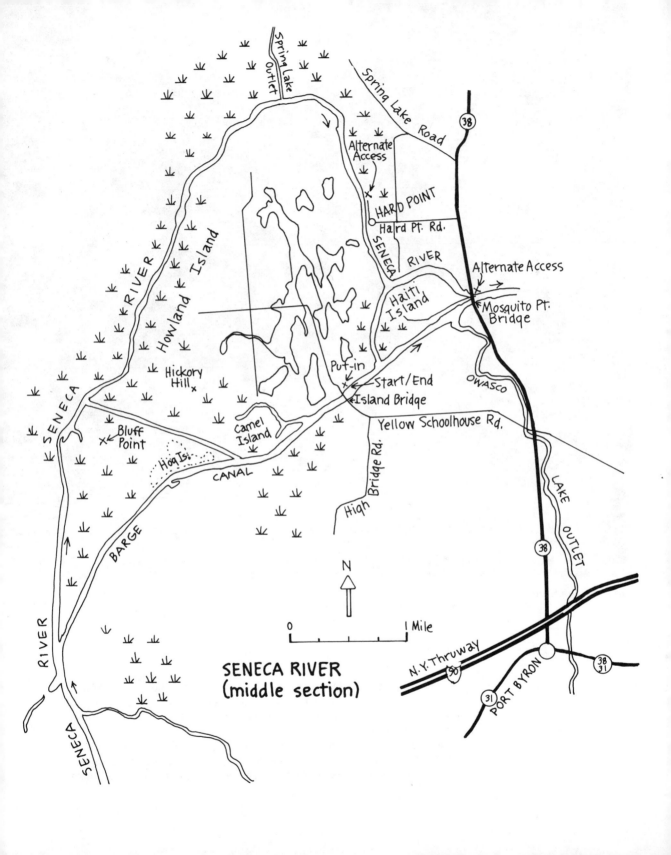

Spring Lake Outlet

Spring Lake Road

(38)

Alternate Access

HARD POINT

Hard Pt. Rd.

SENECA RIVER

Alternate Access

Haiti Island

Mosquito Pt. Bridge

Howland Island

RIVER

SENECA

Hickory Hill ×

Put-in

Start/End
Island Bridge

OWASCO

× Bluff Point

Camel Island

Hog Is.

Yellow Schoolhouse Rd.

SENECA

BARGE CANAL

High Bridge Rd.

LAKE OUTLET

N

0   1 Mile

SENECA RIVER
(middle section)

(38)

N.Y. Thruway (90)

PORT BYRON

(31)

(38 31)

RIVER

SENECA

long and about 2½ miles wide. Like other lakes in the region they drain north, eventually emptying into Lake Ontario, which makes them, along with the Seneca River, part of the St. Lawrence watershed.

Throughout its length the Seneca is a deep, slow-moving waterway, always willing to accommodate the recreational boater. Commercial traffic is only occasionally seen on the Seneca; what you do see is recreational traffic—large and small powerboats, with a good sprinkling of canoes.

The Trip
Start/Launch site on Howland Island

Since the current is barely noticeable you can canoe the Seneca clockwise or counterclockwise. The route for this trip is the latter.

After leaving the launching ramp, head east on the Barge Canal cut. The water is about five canoe lengths wide here and straight as an arrow, with trees gracing both banks.

In less than ½ mile the waterway splits, with the land on the far bank belonging to Haiti Island. A left turn here puts you on Seneca water and heads you back along a northerly loop around Howland Island. The right leg of the split brings you in ¾ mile to Mosquito Point bridge on the Barge Canal. A left turn at the bridge puts you back on the Seneca River and allows you to continue looping Haiti Island as you head north on your route around Howland Island. If you want to shorten your route a bit, just bend left when you first encounter the split.

At this point the land on both sides of the river is low and marshy, but ½ mile upstream the land begins to rise, and another ½ mile brings you to the cluster of homes that makes up the small community of Hard Point at the west end of Hard Point Road.

Although the river here is only half as wide as the barge cut, the water is deep. Woods cover the land on both sides of the river, providing ideal habitat for the area's plentiful birdlife. Another ¾-mile paddle under shady trees brings you to a leftward bend in the river. This is the top of the loop.

A half mile farther on the small stream of Spring Lake Outlet can be seen through some deadfall. This may be the place you stop for a lunch break.

As you start southward on the return part of your trip the woods on both sides become thicker and deeper, but after 1½ miles the trees begin to recede, eventually disappearing altogether on the right side of the stream. Here the land is low and flat and called a savannah (the name, as well, of a nearby town).

End/Launch site on Howland Island

The land is treeless on both sides, now. Soon you see a narrow waterway elbowing off to the left. Follow this route. If you continue straight you will add an additional and, perhaps, a tiring 5-mile loop to your trip. A 1½-mile paddle brings you to the junction with the handsome, tree-lined Barge Canal. In a little over a mile, past tall trees and higher land, you are back at the launching site on Howland Island, having completed a 9-mile circle in about 5 hours of leisurely canoeing.

Alternate Canoe Routes

Since the Seneca is long, the canoeist can find numerous access points which can be used to set up canoe routes of various lengths. While the upper section from Geneva to Seneca Falls is heavily populated, the stretch from Seneca Falls to Howland Island and far downstream to Baldwinsville is virtually wild. On the lower section one again sees signs of civilization on the river's banks.

12

Clyde River

Described Trip:
Lock 26 to Mays Point
7½ miles
Novice at medium high water

Access Points	Interval Distance	Drop and (Gradient)	Trip Time	Water Conditions	Obstacles
River Road Put-in					
	5 miles	2' (0)	2 hours	Slow, flat	Some dead trees
River Road Take-out					
	2	0' (0)	¾	Slow, flat	Some dead trees
Jct. Barge Canal					
	1¼	1' (0)	½	Slow, flat	None
Clyde					
	2½	7' (3)	¾	Slow, flat	None
Lock 26					
	1¼	*0' (0)*	½	*Slow, flat*	*Foot bridge*
Bentley Road					
	2½	*5' (1)*	¾	*Slow, flat*	*Dead trees*
Armitage bridge					
	3½	*1' (0)*	1¼	*Slow, flat*	*None*
Mays Point					
	2	1' (0)	½	Slow, flat	None
Jct. Seneca River					

USGS (7.5') Maps: Lyons, Savannah, Seneca, *Cayuga*

The Clyde River could easily be called New York's version of a southern bayou. The vegetation along the river is lush and dense in late spring and summer, with red maple, ash, and other bottomland trees crowding the river's edge and arching over the water. Wild grape, poison oak, and other vines crawl up trunks and drape themselves around the overhanging limbs, looking for all the world like Spanish moss.

The dark water moves with a slow grace that matches the surrounding solitude. As your canoe glides downstream, a stillness like that of the tropics is broken periodically by the splash of turtles sliding quickly from their sunning places on logs. Ahead, puddle ducks break cover and explode skyward. The almost-submerged trunks of dead trees could, with a little imagination on the canoeist's part, pass for alligators.

The Clyde is a favorite canoeing spot for serious birdwatchers. Overhead, birds of every species found in upstate New York skip and soar through the leafy canopy. Along the water are the herons. Scores of them occupy the river—the great blue heron, the smaller green heron, and even the little blue heron. This is a place where more than 230 species of birds, including rarely sighted varieties such as egret, glossy ibis, Hudsonian godwit, whimbrel, Wilson's phalarope, and Connecticut warbler can be found. That is why members of local Audubon groups go out of their way to search here for species that seem to be found only in inaccessible forest wetlands.

Nonetheless, the Clyde is not for everyone. The water is flat and discolored. Dead trees (probably elms killed years ago by the Dutch elm disease) litter the water, creating a primordial setting. The woods beside the river look impenetrable, even forbidding.

But if you are looking for an unusual, out-of-the-way place, a natural environment that looks unkempt, untouched by man, and that teems with wildlife, the Clyde must be given top billing. If you're a birder, the Clyde's definitely your river; try it during the spring and fall migration periods, when it becomes a sanctuary for nesting, resting, and feeding.

Access   The Clyde River can be reached via NY 31, coming either from Rochester on the west, or from Syracuse on the east; from NY 31 roads run south to the river.

For a day on the lower Clyde, a good take-out is found at Mays Point immediately east of the bridge that carries NY 89 over both the Clyde River and its near neighbor, the Barge Canal, and into the northern portion of the Montezuma National Wildlife Refuge. There is room to park a half dozen cars next to the bridge.

The suggested put-in spot is Lock 26 on the Barge Canal, just east of Clyde village. As the map shows, the Barge and the Clyde come together and separate, so part of your canoe trip is on the Barge and part on the Clyde. In the village turn south, cross the bridge over the canal, and turn left onto Redfield Street. Follow this street until it merges with Glover Road, which runs south past Lock Road.

Turn left onto Lock Road and follow it for a mile, passing a gravel pit, to the Barge Canal, and finally to Lock 26. Running across the canal from the lock is a six-foot-high dam. Check in with the lockkeeper. He'll tell you where to park, and he can also tell you the best put-in spot at the lock. He may even allow you

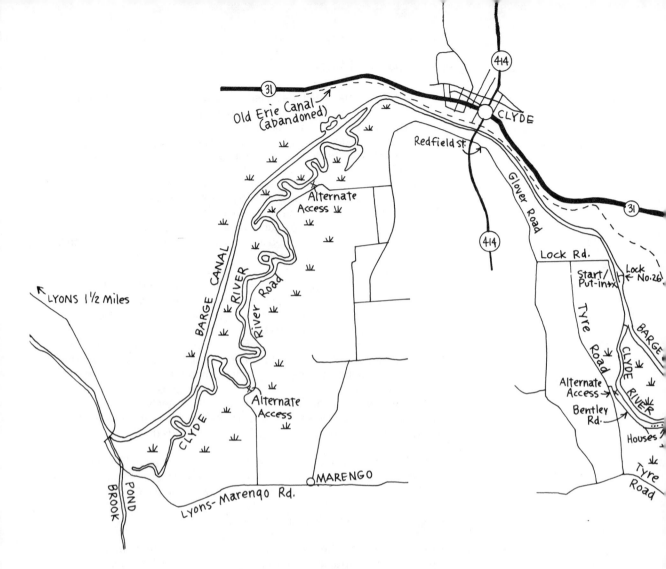

and your group to pass through the lock with your canoes, by letting you put in at the lock's north end. Otherwise, you put in at the downstream side of the lock, but below the concrete embankment.

The River   The Clyde acts as if it had nowhere to go—with good reason, considering the way it is sandwiched among several other waterways that almost rob it of its place and personality.

To begin with, there's the Barge Canal. When it was built at the beginning of the present century it did much to change the Clyde—to some extent its course of flow, much of its character, and surely its origin. Before the Barge, the junction of the Garnagua Creek (see Trip 14) and the Canadaigua Outlet (see Trip 13) at what today is the village of Lyons marked the start of the Clyde. From here the river made its way eastward for 23 miles through marshy bottomland, eventually reaching the Seneca River just north of Cayuga Lake.

With the construction of the Barge Canal, however, the waters of the Garnagua and Canadaigua were diverted to the canal, letting the upper portion of the Clyde fend for itself. In the lower portion the Clyde was, in part, incorporated into the Barge system.

Now, about 3 miles east of Lyons, you find the presentday beginning of the Clyde. It is a watery, dead end ditch filled with fallen dead trees, wholly impassable and thoroughly unattractive. Clearly the Clyde came on hard times; even Pond Brook, which once fed into the Clyde, now bypasses the Clyde and flows northeast to empty into the Barge.

However, as you move downstream conditions begin to improve, and the Clyde starts to look more like its old self, looping back and forth through the thinly populated town of Galen for 10 miles before merging with the Barge. For a while the Clyde and the Barge are one, but soon the Clyde strikes out on its own, only to rejoin the Barge downstream. It does this several more times before it finally breaks free to flow into the Seneca River.

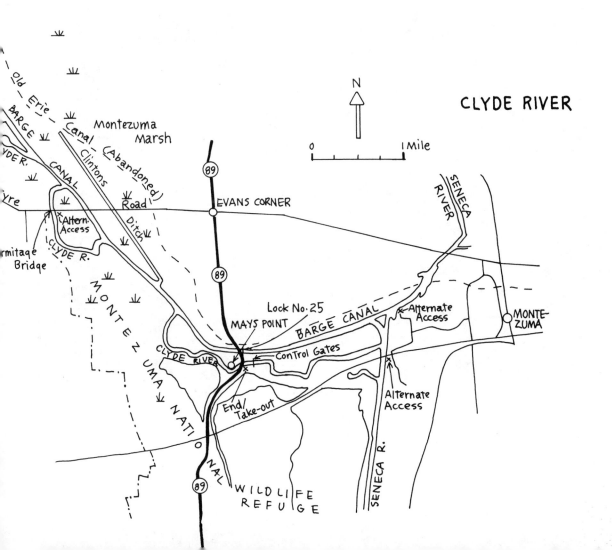

CLYDE RIVER

Carrying past Lock 26 on Barge Canal to put-in point.

The Trip At Lock 26 the put-in is, of course, on the Barge, which is flat, wide, and deep. A
Start/Lock 26 half mile past fields and tree-lined banks brings you to the Clyde River,
bending off the Barge on the right. A short distance down the Clyde you
encounter a causeway across the river, part of which is a wooden walk bridge
over a low dam. Drag your canoe over the causeway to the other side and
continue your journey.

Trees along this first loop begin to thicken into woods; the number of dead
trees in the water also increases. Soon on your right is Bentley Road, one of the
alternate put-in spots along the river. On your left is a thickly wooded island
made by the Barge and the Clyde.

Ahead is a red buoy, marking the intersection of the Clyde and the Barge. A
short distance down the canal the Clyde separates for its second loop, again
on the right. Here the deadfall in the water is thick; on occasion you have to
push floating logs aside to get through. You can avoid this by canoeing the
Barge, but if you do you'll also miss seeing birdlife such as the herons who
prefer the Clyde.

Back again on the Barge, you now have ½ mile to go to the Clyde's third loop,
again on the right. This stretch brings you in little less than ½ mile to Armitage
bridge, an alternate take-out spot. This loop is a bit more scenic than the last
one, with hardly any downed trees to mar the aquatic setting.

End/Mays Point The Clyde's last loop—1½ miles in length—is a relatively attractive section
with tall trees gracing both riverbanks. Soon you can spot the NY 89 bridge
ahead, and as you approach you see on your left Mays Point, a community of
about two dozen houses. Farther downriver are the gates that control the
waterflow into, and the level of, the Barge itself. About 50 yards more brings
you to your take-out.

Alternate One option is the upper section of the Clyde which follows a course indepen-
Canoe Routes dent of the canal, and which is by far the more primitive portion of the Clyde.
Running next to the Clyde most of the way is River Road. Your put-in is the
place where the road touches the river for the first time in the upper reaches,
and your take-out is where the road touches the river for the last time in the
lower reaches—a distance of 5 miles.

Still another route is the one running for 2 miles from Mays Point to the
junction with the Seneca River. There's one take-out by a dirt road south of the
Clyde's junction with the Seneca, and another on the right at the junction of the
Seneca and the Barge Canal.

13

Canandaigua Outlet

Described Trip:
Phelps to Alloway
10 miles
Novice at medium water
Intermediate at medium high water

Access Points	Interval Distance	Drop and (Gradient)	Trip Time	Water Conditions	Obstacles
Canandaigua Lake					
	4 miles	4' (1)	1¼ hours	Flat/slow	None
Chapin					
	4	66' (17)	1	Very fast	Some debris
Shortsville					
	1½	70' (35)	¾	Very fast	Drops; rapids
NY 96 bridge					
	6	50' (8)	2	Moderate	None
Gypsum					
	5½	23' (4)	2	Moderate	None
Phelps					
	2½	*37' (15)*	*½*	*Moderate*	*None*
Pre-Emption Rd. bridge					
	4	*20' (5)*	*1¼*	*Moderate*	*Debris in left channel*
Gifford Rd. bridge					
	2¼	*10' (3)*	*½*	*Moderate*	*None*
Alloway					
	3	25' (8)	1	Moderate	Dam
Lyons					

USGS (7.5') Maps: Canandaigua, Clifton Springs, Phelps, Geneva North, Lyons

The Canandaigua Outlet's lower half from Phelps to Alloway could easily be called the river of tall trees—with red maple, oak, ash, and especially willow and cottonwood soaring skyward from the riverbanks to heights of five and six stories. In late spring and early summer, when the trees are in full foliage, the water flows through a gorge of green, producing as picturesque a setting as you can find in central New York.

That is just one of the Canandaigua Outlet's attractions. In addition, the river can be described as clear, clean, and free—bottom-seeing clear for almost its entire length, remarkably clean of deadfall and debris, and pleasantly free of rocks and other obstacles.

Most important, the water moves at a nice pace—a pace that makes paddling hardly necessary and the day's float a joy to remember.

As its name indicates, the stream is the outlet of Canandaigua Lake. To the Indians, Canandaigua meant "the chosen place," or "place selected for settlement." The larger region around the outlet is indeed settled and prosperous-looking, but along the stream itself there is little evidence of civilization, except for Shortsville, Manchester, and Phelps.

Much of the visual appeal of this river comes from the unusual variety to be found in its natural setting. As you canoe past the tall trees, they change —stretches of willow, then red oak, to be followed by cottonwood. In late May and early June, when the cottonwood releases its feathery seedlings, it "snows" on the Canadaigua Outlet—small white, cottony tufts drift down, coming to rest by the hundreds on the water and on passing canoes.

Below, through the clear water, you can see an abundance of aquatic plants bending and swaying in the current. Even these change from one mile to the next: here you see milfoil, and then hornwort ("coontail"), and so on, as you glide over more than a half dozen different species.

Along the banks there are memorable, successive sights—large patches of ostrich fern standing tall and regal in the sunlight, or long, thick stretches of purple and white phlox gracing your passage with color.

Access   Your take-out point is found on the southwest side of the bridge at the western edge of Alloway, a hamlet located on NY 14, 3 miles south of Lyons, and 5 miles north of NY 14's intersection with the New York Thruway (I-90). A short path leads from the water to the road, where there is room to park several vehicles.

A good spot to start your trip is the village of Phelps, on NY 96, about 7 miles northwest of Geneva on Seneca Lake, and near the midpoint of the outlet. In Phelps, turn north on North Wayne Street and follow it, along with Flint Creek, to the bridge. There is room here to park. A path on the northeast side of the bridge brings you to the water and your put-in spot.

The Outlet   The outlet is a moderately fast-flowing stream, with its lower half a bit wider than a creek and somewhat smaller than a river. In this section from Phelps to Alloway the water depth in late spring remains around 3 feet, deepening a little more as you approach Lyons, where the outlet empties into the Barge Canal. Before the Barge was built the outlet was a tributary of the Clyde River (see Trip 12).

As the outlet flows from Canandaigua Lake to Lyons, its 36-mile length stretches in an S-shaped course over the northern portion of Ontario County and the southern part of Wayne County. An attractive feature of this waterway is that its entire length is canoeable, as it runs first north to Shortsville and Manchester, then eastward for 16 miles, and finally north again for 10 miles to Lyons.

From Canandaigua Lake to Chapin the land is relatively high and flat; here the water moves slowly. Then it starts a fast, almost whitewater, run to Shortsville, tumbling down the escarpment toward the Lake Ontario lowlands, dropping more than 135 feet in 5¼ miles for a substantial gradient of 25. Below Manchester, however, on its way to Lyons, the stream slows to a moderate velocity, making this lower section the more canoed route with a gradient of only 7.

The Trip
Start/North Wayne Street bridge

As you put in at the North Wayne Street bridge, the current is moving at a moderate speed—the speed the outlet will maintain for virtually your entire trip. As you paddle downstream you are immediately greeted by tall trees on both sides of the stream, trees which appear to grow even taller as you proceed. Occasionally a break appears in the tree line, allowing you to see nearby fields atop small, rolling hills.

At 2½ miles you approach your first bridge, Pre-Emption Road. If you put into

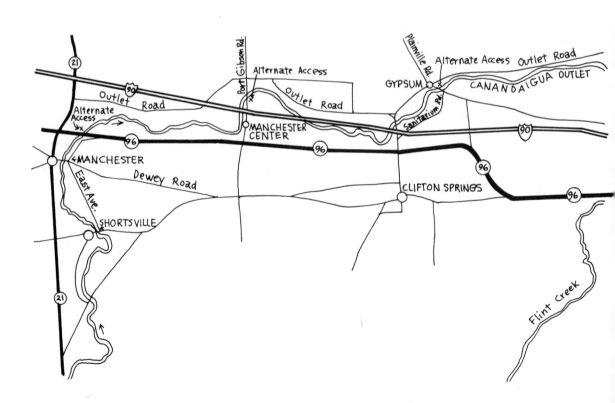

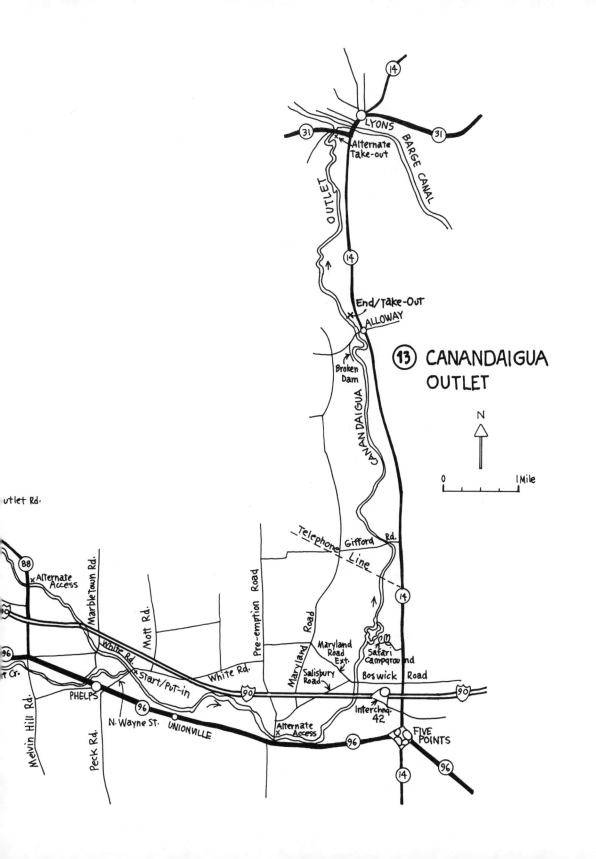

13 CANANDAIGUA OUTLET

N

0   1 Mile

the water just before noon (which is often the case if you've had a long drive to the put-in), the northeast side of this bridge is a good spot to put ashore for a lunch break.

As you continue your journey downstream you notice after a mile that the stream is bending slowly to the left, to head on its finally northward course. Now you hear vehicles and then you see the Thruway (I-90) bridge; just ahead is still another bridge, this one is Boswick Road.

About ¾ mile downstream from Boswick Road, the stream splits to create several sizeable islands. The left channel tends to get cluttered with debris, so stay in the right channel which is normally clear of deadfall. As you enter this channel you start to see parked trailers on your right, indicating you are passing the Safari Campgrounds, a private establishment and a place you might use if you are making a weekend of it.

Beyond the campgrounds the stream comes together again, continuing its northward course in a series of barely noticeable turns. A mile from the campgrounds, a telephone cable can be seen stretching almost at treetop level over the stream, and ½ mile more finds you at Gifford Road bridge.

The next 3 miles is a leisurely float with the stream deepening and widening a bit; about ¾ of your way down this section the stream suddenly cuts sharply to the left, and runs a short but fast loop before widening and slowing again.

End/Alloway bridge

Then ahead you see what is left of an old dam; the concrete part still stands, but the water makes its way slowly through a large break or washout on the right side. The stream now swings gently to the right, and then begins a loop back again, with the water speeding up to give you a farewell treat—a nice run for several hundred yards as you approach your take-out spot. Ferry across the stream and put ashore on the southwest side of the bridge, where you'll probably see some youngsters fishing.

Alternate Canoe Routes

You can, of course, start at Canandaigua Lake, where you might first want to do some canoe sailing. From the lake it is 4 miles to Chapin. Take out here if you want to avoid the fast drop to Shortsville. If you plan to run this fast section, check it out first.

In the lower section, a good put-in is at the NY 96 bridge on the northern edge of Manchester. From here you have moderately fast water for 6 miles to Gypsum (which can also be a put-in spot); 5½ more miles brings you to the first bridge in Phelps.

The route from Alloway to Lyons is 3 miles. Take out by the road on your left, about a hundred yards before you reach the NY 31 bridge.

14

Ganargua Creek

Described Trip:
NY 88 to Lyons
9 miles
Novice at medium water
Intermediate at medium high water

Access Points	Interval Distance	Drop and (Gradient)	Trip Time	Water Conditions	Obstacles
Swift Landing Park					
	8 miles	10' (1)	2½ hours	Moderately fast, chute	Small dam, low spot, downed trees
NY 88 bridge					
	2	*5' (2)*	*1*	*Moderately fast, two chutes*	*Some debris, downed trees*
Mud Mills bridge					
	2	*6' (3)*	*¾*	*Moderately fast*	*Some debris*
Narsen Bridge Park					
	5	*10' (2)*	*1 ½*	*Slow, flat*	*Some debris*
Abbey Park at Lyons					

USGS (7.5') Maps: Palmyra, Newark

Getting ready to canoe the Ganargua.

The Ganargua is a lively, winsome little waterway that appeals to the canoeist through his muscles as well as through his eyes. One of the creek's assets is its active water—it runs full all season, with the kind of movement that makes canoeists, especially during the dry of summer, eager to put paddle to water and feel the push of the current.

The Ganargua's main water source is the Barge Canal at a point just east of Palmyra. The canal manages to supply the creek with all the water it needs to make it a fast-flowing stream for almost two-thirds of its length. As bonuses, the Ganargua also offers several chutes along the way—short, fast drops that can be run for added excitement.

As for the creek's appearance: lining the banks for its entire length are tall trees whose thick limbs arch gracefully over the water to touch hands with their cousins on the other side. The ash trees are particularly given to this posture as they literally form half circles, as if bowing to a lady fair.

The Ganargua appears to enjoy presenting examples of every kind of tree in this Lake Ontario region, which extends from Syracuse to Rochester, and from Lake Ontario south to the Finger Lakes Hills. There are trees that like the savannahs, bottomlands, and wetlands—willow, cottonwood, aspen, ash, red maple, and basswood; but also in numbers are walnut, butternut, shagbark hickory, oak, beech, and sycamore.

Sometimes the Ganargua mixes them together. Other times it displays only one species for a particular stretch. But whatever its arrangement, the scenery is a delight to the eye.

Also, this seems to be the summer residence of the cedar waxwings. In June you can see them by the hundreds along the creek, flitting through the tall trees and darting across the water. Even the great blue heron appears to be in league with the Ganargua, acting as the stream's resident heron and posing for the canoeist—waiting, tall and dignified, until the canoe comes almost abreast, before it lifts off and flies a short distance downstream to wait again.

The Ganargua flows through a land that once belonged to the Cayuga and Seneca Indians. The completion of the Erie Canal in 1825 brought a rapid growth of villages—or canal towns—such as Lyons, Newark, and Palmyra, and with this population growth came new social issues and a new religious ferment. Joseph Smith's vision on the Hill of Cumorah near Palmyra resulted in the Book of Mormon and the founding of the Church of Jesus Christ of Latter-day Saints. The home of the Fox sisters near Hydesville is regarded as the "birthplace of spiritualism."

Geographically, the Ganargua area is rural. Geologically, it is situated in what is known as the Ontario drumlin region, where hundreds of drumlins —glacially produced hills—can be found, usually in groups that the geologists call "swarms." Agriculturally, the area is known for its fruit orchards and horticultural nurseries, especially for the growing of roses.

Access
The principal access route is NY 31, which follows the Barge Canal between Syracuse and Rochester. Paved roads are found on both sides of the Ganargua.

The best take-out spot is found at Abbey Park on the west side of Lyons, at the junction of the Ganargua and the Barge Canal. To reach the park, take Lyons

Road west out of Lyons for several city blocks. The park is on the left side of the road.

A number of put-in spots can be found along the Ganargua. The recommended one is found where NY 88 crosses the creek, just a mile north of where NY 88 and NY 31 intersect in the center of Newark. Here you'll find convenient access points; you can put in at any side of the bridge. The best spot, however, is on the northeast side, where a dirt lane runs the short distance from the highway to the water's edge. Here, the creek's banks are low and the water moves slowly.

The Creek When the Barge Canal was constructed, the engineers changed the flow pattern of a number of streams along the route. In some cases they took water away from existing waterways such as the Clyde River (see Trip 12); in others they fed canal water into existing streams, making them run fuller than before—the Ganargua is one of these.

About two miles east of Palmyra is a story-high overflow dam on the Barge Canal. The source of the Ganargua is the excess water that spills over this dam. From this spot the creek swings north into the first of two large loops, following

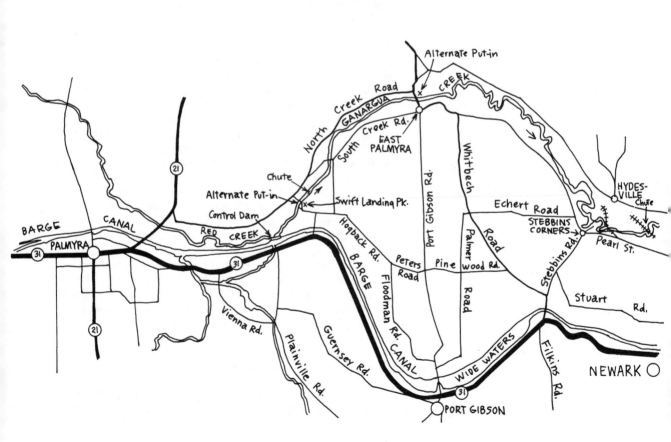

a course above the canal, for a 17-mile journey to Lyons. There it ends by flowing back into the Barge.

Because the Barge Canal has more water than it needs, the Ganaragua is a busy stream. The color of the creek's water is the same as that of the Barge —murky and, after a rain, on the coffee-colored side. Apart from this color, the Ganargua gives the paddler what he most desires—fast-flowing water.

The creek can conveniently be divided in half. The upper section runs from Swift Landing Park near the canal dam, to the bridge in the north of Newark, covering a distance of 8 miles; the lower section runs 9 miles from Newark to

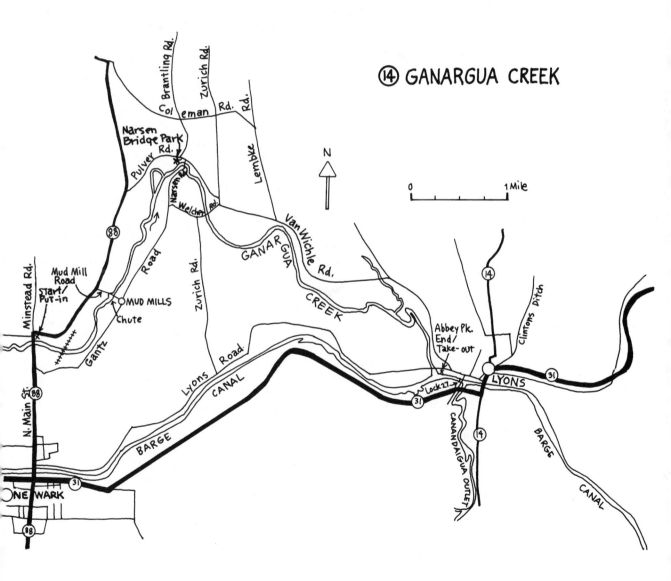

⑭ GANARGUA CREEK

Lyons. Each of these sections is one of the loops above the Barge Canal; together, the loops form a lazy "M."

There are dead trees and blowdowns in the creek, giving rise to debris pileups; you may have to carry around these obstacles. Look for tree blockage coming out of East Palmyra and also about a mile downstream from Stebbins Corners.

The Trip
Start/Northeast side at NY 88 bridge

As the Ganargua reaches the NY 88 bridge, it widens and slows, making your put-in relatively easy. The creek's main channel is on the right side; so head for it and begin your trip. Once past the bridge, the creek narrows and deepens again. You may find some debris along the route but not enough to obstruct passage.

Keep in mind that the water rises several feet in late spring and late fall. Sometimes high water washes out the debris but at other times the high water can undercut trees, thereby creating obstacles and strainers.

A little over a mile downstream from the NY 88 bridge you come to Mud Mills Road bridge and a chute just beyond the highway bridge; it is found near the middle of the stream with the channel a little to the right. If you try it on the left when the creek is low, you'll scrape bottom. The chute can be run by novices but with care. It is best to have an experienced paddler aboard. If you are uncertain line your canoe through the chute.

From Mud Mills it is a 2-mile paddle to Narsen Bridge Park—a nice place to stop for a lunch break. Look through the trees on your left for the park buildings. Picnic tables, water, and restrooms are available here.

As soon as you are back in the water you pass under the new Narsen Road bridge; the old one collapsed into the river in 1986. From here the creek flows in a southeasterly direction, making a series of slow loops. When you are a little less than a mile from the park you pass under Welcher Road bridge, the last bridge before Lyons.

End/Abbey Park at Lyons

The Ganargua begins both to widen and to slow a bit in this lower section. About a mile north of Lyons the creek makes a tight "S." You make a sharp turn to your left, and you are actually canoeing northward parallel to the section you just paddled; another sharp turn to your right results in a repeat performance going the other way. But now the creek runs a straight course southward, and soon you see signs of civilization—a large farm on your left, and then houses in increasing numbers. Ahead is the Lyons Road bridge, and immediately afterward on the Barge Canal side is the Abbey Park take-out.

Alternate Canoe Routes

An obvious alternate route is the upper section of the Ganargua, starting at Swift Landing Park and ending at the NY 88 bridge north of Newark. Other possibilities include canoeing sections of the Barge Canal between Palmyra and Lyons. You can also combine the Ganargua and the Barge Canal; try putting in at Narsen Bridge Park, canoeing on the Ganargua to Lyons, and then on the Barge to Newark.

Ontario Lake—
St. Lawrence Watershed
(North Flow)

15

Mudge Creek/East Bay

Described Trip:
Garner Road Launch Site and back
6 miles
Beginner at medium high water

Access Points	Interval Distance	Drop and (Gradient)	Trip Time	Water Conditions	Obstacles
West bridge Launch Site					
	1¼ miles	0' (0)	½ hour	Stillwater	None
East bridge					
	2½	0' (0)	¾	Flatwater	None
North Huron bridge					
	3	0' (0)	1	Flatwater	None
East Bay Park					
	2	0' (0)	¾	Stillwater	None
West bridge					

USGS (7.5') Maps: Rose, Sodus Point.

Lunch break.

The Mudge Creek/East Bay area is a place of elongated drumlins, soaring bluffs, meandering wetlands, landlocked bays, backwater streams, waterfowl and shorebirds. Here the canoeist can enjoy a mixture of water and landscape that is both gentle and unusual.

It is gentle in that its low, rolling terrain is covered by cultivated fields and small wood stands, and its canoeable water has virtually no drop.

But just down the road from the community of East Bay Park, Chimney Bluff leaps up 150 feet from the shore of Lake Ontario—an unusual bluff of sand and gravel that has been carved by natural forces into a cluster of cathedral-like pinnacles joined by saddles, many of which are as sharp as knives. It is a breathtaking sight from the top or from below.

Also unusual is the landlocked bay. There are several along this part of the Lake Ontario shore. East Bay is one of the largest. They really aren't bays, since their mouths are sealed off; they are more like ponds, except that they are part of a stream system. The action of wind-driven waves rolls up sand and small stones at a stream outlet, forming a narrow land strip which acts as a dam, making a "bay" that holds water that has nowhere to go, even though Lake Ontario is only a few yards away.

And the hills in this area are really drumlins, shaped like loaves of pumpernickel bread. The axis of elongated drumlins always runs north and south. You can tell the north end because on the north the hill's slope is more pronounced than it is on the south.

The canoeing possibilities here are many. If you want to do some ordinary flatwater paddling, Mudge Creek and East Bay can accommodate you with 7 miles of canoeable water. Exploring all the tributaries and returning to your start will more than double that mileage.

If you want to canoe-pole you can try the upper reaches of Mudge Creek and East Bay's other tributaries. Canoe sailing? There is no better place than East Bay to unfurl a sail. Angling from a canoe? There are plenty of fish on which to try your spin-casting or fly-casting skills. Picnicking and swimming, perhaps? You'll find some nice spots on a beach that you can easily reach by canoe. Bird-watching? Come in the spring and you'll be occupied all day identifying birds and waterfowl from your canoe.

In short, these waters compensate for their gentleness by providing the conditions for a variety of canoe activities and the fun of exploring a wetland wildlife sanctuary.

Access   The waters are immediately adjacent to Lake Ontario at a point about half way between Syracuse and Rochester. On your road map find Wolcott, southeast of Mudge Creek and East Bay, and just north of US 104.

From Wolcott, take the main road west out of town. A mile from the center of Wolcott, the road forks. Bear to your right and drive 5.2 miles to Lake Bluff Road. Turn north here. At .8 mile, Lake Bluff Road turns left, but Garner Road continues due north. Follow Garner Road; at the 2-mile mark it will turn east and then head south to cross over a tributary to East Bay at the 1.2-mile mark.

Let's call this the west bridge. Park in an area on the east side of the road by the water's edge. Here is both your take-out and your put-in point.

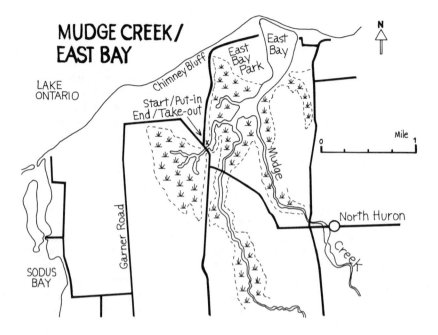

The Water East Bay, which is 1¼ miles long, and ½ mile wide at its far end, is fed by
several tributaries of which Mudge Creek is the principal feeder stream. On the
topo map the four tributaries look like the root system of a tree. Two drain the
wetland area in the west and north. The other two, one of which is Mudge Creek,
have their headquarters far to the south of the marshland.

The source of Mudge Creek is 10½ miles south, near Stewart Corners. As the
creek flows north it widens and deepens into a sizeable pond south of the
hamlet of North Huron, the effect of a dam just south of North Huron's main road.
One-and-a-half miles above North Huron, Mudge Creek empties into East Bay.

These waters are difficult to classify. Technically, "flatwater" means moving
water in rivers and streams. Since Mudge Creek is a slow-moving, smooth-
flowing stream we can speak of its water as flatwater. In East Bay one finds
stillwater, so East Bay has to be classified as one would a lake. The best option
may be to call all of it simply backwater.

In any event, it is water ideally suited to the beginner and to family canoeists.
In the spring Mudge rises a bit, but it never reaches the quick or fastwater
stage. Spring and early summer are good times to canoe these waters, when
pond weeds haven't grown enough to clog the feeder streams' upper sections.
Then one can also see both migratory and native birds as they go into their
mating and nesting rituals.

The main marsh area and the land on both sides of the feeder streams are
state-owned and are supervised by New York State's Department of Environ-

mental Conservation. They are identified by the DEC as the East Bay Marsh Unit, and are open to hunters in the fall during waterfowl season. To the north, adjoining the DEC's marshland, is more state land, including all of the Chimney Bluff area, which is operated by the state's Parks and Recreation Commission. Only the lower end of East Bay is surrounded by private land.

The Trip
Start/West bridge

The water at the put-in point is flat and several canoe-lengths wide. Once you've shoved off, head downstream in a northeasterly direction.

Since this is a popular fishing spot, you will probably see fishermen lining the left shore. The land on that side rises sharply forming a small tree-covered hill. On the right the land is flat and treeless. After ½ mile you enter the wetland area with its tall grasses and cattails. You also encounter the outlet of a feeder stream.

Follow it southward, paddling upstream in a current you can hardly feel. The marsh area begins to narrow considerably now, rarely getting much wider than the stream itself. A half mile brings you to the east bridge, where the land narrows and rises to form a hill on your left. Continue upstream, if you like, for another 1¼ miles. If you brought your canoe pole you can start using it now to get some additional mileage.

Paddle back and head for East Bay. Stay on the right side of the water, and in ¼ mile you will notice another stream outlet. This is Mudge Creek. Follow it upstream as it passes through a narrow stretch running about a mile between two tree-covered drumlins. You can do some poling as you near North Huron. When the water gets too shallow, reverse direction and head back to East Bay.

By now you should have seen a variety of birds—probably five or six species of ducks, a couple of herons, several different kinds of shorebirds, and an impressive number of smaller land birds.

End/West bridge

As you enter East Bay you will paddle through the neck before the water opens wide, showing you that you are in the main bay. Another ½ mile brings you to the narrow beach, about 5 yards wide, which has closed the bay's mouth. You can carry over this land strip and put into Lake Ontario, or you can swing back on your return route, passing a community of homes called East Bay Park on the west side of the bay. From here it is about 2 miles back to the west bridge and your take-out point.

Alternate Canoe Routes

In these waters it is just a matter of deciding which channels and feeder streams to explore. The two principal tributaries stretch southward, each with about 2 miles of easily canoeable water.

When Lake Ontario is calm, as it usually is in summer, you can paddle along the lakeshore to the east or to the west.

Another option is to try Sodus Bay, just 2 miles west of your put-in site. Sodus Bay is large—2½ miles wide at its mouth, and 3¼ miles long. It is a popular spot for canoe sailing.

16

Sterling Creek

Described Trip:
Fraden Road bridge to Lake Ontario
7½ miles
Novice at medium water

Access Points	Interval Distance	Drop and (Gradient)	Trip Time	Water Conditions	Obstacles
EAST BRANCH					
Sterling Valley					
	1 mile	1' (1)	⅓ hour	Fastwater, riffles	None
Old State Road					
	1	1' (1)	⅓	Flatwater	None
Fraden Road					
	1	*1' (1)*	*⅓*	*Flatwater*	*None*
McIntrye Road					
	½	*2' (4)*	*¼*	*Flatwater*	*None*
Jct. West Branch					
WEST BRANCH					
Onionville Road					
	1	1' (1)	⅓	Fastwater	Dam
Sterling					
	1 ½	*20' (13)*	*½*	*Flatwater, riffles*	*None*
Old State Road					
	1	*4' (1)*	*¼*	*Flatwater*	*None*
Jct. East Branch					
STERLING (MAIN STEM)					
Junction					
	1 ½	*1' (0)*	*½*	*Flatwater*	*None*
Sterling Pond					
	½	*0' (0)*	*¼*	*Stillwater*	*None*
Lake Ontario					

USGS (7.5") Maps: Hannibal, Victory, Fair Haven.

Save Sterling Creek for springtime when the world comes alive again, when the birds have migrated back to mate and nest, and the land is covered with a soft yellow-green, heralding the coming of summer. At this time, before the pond-weeds and algae take over, the waterways run free and clean.

Although both the main stem of the Sterling and its two branches can be described as quietwater—livewater in its upper reaches and stillwater in the lower—the creek has its sounds, such as the dancing of water on rocks and gravel beds and the lapping of waves in rushes. To these are added the music of songbirds, the grunting arias of frogs, and the rustling of wind through marsh grass, composing a happy symphony which gives Sterling Creek its special flavor and makes many canoeists plan to return.

If you like variety in your canoeing experiences and are making your first trip to Sterling, you are in for some pleasant surprises. Canoe polers should head for the upper stretches. Fishermen will find the creek's water filled with game fish, including huge trout running upstream from Lake Ontario. Birdwatchers will have lots to discover in a section of the creek called the Moat. If you are a canoe sailor, the stream's lower end at Sterling Pond is the place for you.

When you canoe the Sterling, make a weekend of it and stay at Fair Haven State Park, through which the creek flows. Here you can camp and picnic, enjoy the wide sandy beach, and, when the weather is warm enough, take a refreshing swim in Lake Ontario.

Access   Sterling Creek lies east of the village of Fair Haven, which is located on the southeast end of Little Sodus Bay, a mile south of Lake Ontario. There are a number of easily reached access spots to Sterling Creek at its mouth in Fair Haven State Park, and along the middle sections of both creek branches.

The suggested take-out spot is in Fair Haven State Park. Follow the road north into the park, past the toll booth, around the pond (crossing the bridge over the outlet), and past the beach area to a large parking lot where you can leave vehicles. The take-out site is back at the pond, near the outlet.

A way to proceed to the put-in is to take NY 104A out of Fair Haven and travel east for .5 mile to a fork where NY 104A bears to the right and Old State Road bears to the left. NY 104A crosses Sterling Creek in the hamlet of Sterling just 2.4 miles down the road. There's a possible put-in spot here if you can negotiate the steep bank below the dam, and another just north of Sterling.

If you take Old State Road at the fork, .2 mile brings you to a bridge crossing Sterling Creek. It is easy to launch a canoe here, to go either upstream or downstream. However, you will find even better put-in spots a bit farther along.

Cross the bridge and continue on Old State Road for .3 mile, turn left onto Center Road, and drive .8 mile to where the road forks. McIntyre Road goes left and crosses the creek at .4 mile, while Fraden Road bears right and crosses the creek at .8 mile. Fraden Road bridge is the recommended put-in point.

The Creek   The creek is situated in an attractive countryside filled with what geologists call "swarms" of drumlins—small, half-egg-shaped hills produced by the glacier's southward advance 12,000 years ago. There are many hundreds of drumlins in this part of New York, more than can be found anywhere else in the East.

The headwaters of the Sterling are found fifteen miles south of Lake Ontario in two branches only two-and-a-half miles apart. These two streams parallel each other as they run north. Just before reaching Lake Ontario they both loop in a northwesterly direction and join to form a surprisingly broad and deep waterway which looks more like a river than a creek. This main stem now snakes to the southwest, flowing through a fairly large wetland area, past the southern side of Fair Haven Park, and into Sterling Pond. A cut through the narrow beach which separates the pond from Lake Ontario allows the water to flow into the lake.

There is some disagreement as to what the two branches are called. On the USGS Fair Haven topo map one branch is called Sterling Valley Creek, while the other is called Sterling Creek. But signs at bridges over the former say East Branch. Local people refer to the two creeks as the East Branch and the West Branch; we shall follow this custom.

STERLING CREEK

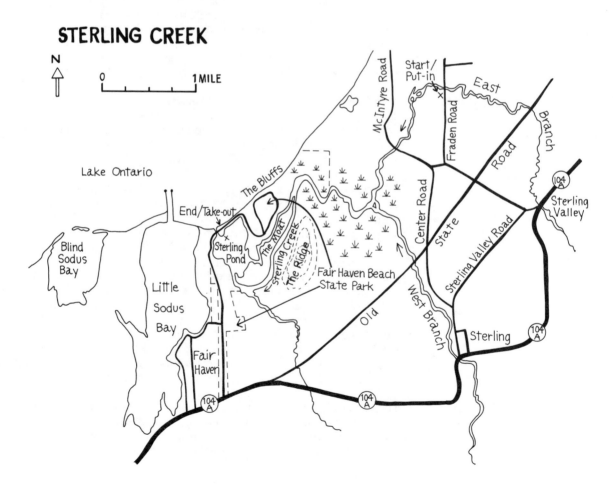

Greenery along Sterling Creek.

The East Branch starts about a mile northwest to Bethel Corners and, as a narrow creek, flows northward for 9 miles to a dam in the hamlet of Sterling Valley. From the dam to the junction with the West Branch is 4½ miles. Only the lower 2 miles of the 14-mile-long East Branch is canoeable, although in early spring you can squeeze more miles out of the upper section if you resort to poling.

The West Branch starts 2½ miles southeast of Victory, and runs 11½ miles north to a dam in Martville. Downstream another 3½ miles is a second dam at Sterling; this section can be canoed if you are ready to duck barbed wire and drag your canoe over riffles. Canoeing on the West Branch is most promising from Sterling to the junction with the East Branch, about 1½ miles downstream.

It is 2 miles from the junction to Lake Ontario, with an interesting split in the stream in the lower section, providing a canoeable alternative to Sterling Creek that hugs the park's southern hillside and is called the Moat.

The Trip
Start/Fraden Road bridge

The best place to start is Fraden Road bridge. The bank to the creek is not very steep, so you'll be in the water in a matter of minutes. Here the rural countryside is dotted with small farms and grazing land interspersed with small wood stands.

The East Branch, clean and clear, runs straight in a westerly direction for about ½ mile before looping southward to enter a wetland area where the creek splits into a figure eight. It quickly straightens out and hurries southward past wood stands on both sides of the creek. The woods move back as you pass under the McIntyre Road bridge.

The East Branch now flows through a narrow valley between two drumlins. As you clear the end of the hill on your right, the East Branch and the West Branch join. You have to choose between continuing on Sterling's main stem, or canoeing upstream on the West Branch. Try the West Branch; it is easy paddling.

From here to the hamlet of Sterling, a distance of only 1½ miles, the tree-lined West Branch passes through attractive drumlin country. You will be able to enjoy this scenery even more, of course, during your float back to the junction.

By the time you reach the junction you will be deep in the heart of the marshland with its miles of tall grass and cattails. For the next mile the Sterling moves slowly, making a couple of lazy turns as it goes. Beyond the marsh, on the right and on the left, are appealing, tree-covered drumlins.

The Sterling now swings to the left, moving into a narrow cut between two drumlins, a high spot on the left called The Ridge, and one on the right occupied by Fair Haven State Park. Just as the loop straightens out you can see the Moat angling off on the right.

End/Fair Haven State Park

Continue on Sterling for the next 1½ miles until you enter Sterling Pond. If you want to do some bird watching, bend to your right, find the Moat's outlet at the edge of the park, and follow it upstream. With a good pair of binoculars you ought to log members of two dozen species without difficulty. The Moat is tree-strewn but it is not difficult to canoe. In the spring you can easily see carp bunched up in their annual mating ritual, suddenly darting about as your canoe passes by. When you are finished you can take out at Fair Haven State Park anywhere along Sterling Pond.

Alternate Canoe Routes

On a calm day you can canoe Lake Ontario to see the Bluffs, high drumlins cut back by wind, rain, and water, which run northeastward from Fair Haven State Park for four miles. The most spectacular, Sitts Bluff and McIntyres Bluff, are worth viewing from Lake Ontario.

The canoe sailor also should take note of 2-mile-long Little Sodus Bay right next to Sterling Pond, and, a little farther west, the mile-long Blind Sodus Bay. Both bays are ideal for canoe sailing or just plain flatwater paddling.

17

Oswego River/Ox Creek

Described Trip:
Phoenix to County Route 14 bridge
10½ miles
Novice at medium water

Access Points	Interval Distance	Drop and (Gradient)	Trip Time	Water Conditions	Obstacles
Three Rivers					
	2½ miles	1' (0)	1 hour	Flat	None
Phoenix (Lock No. 1)					
	3	1' (0)	1	Flat	None
Walter Island					
	1	4' (4)	⅓	Flat	None
Hinmansville					
	1¼	0' (0)	½	Flat	None
Great Bear Rec. Area					
	1¼	0' (0)	½	Flat	None
Jct. Ox Creek					
	2	4' (2)	¾	Flat	None
County Rt. 14 bridge					
	1¼	4' (3)	½	Flat	Some debris
S. Granby Rd. bridge					
	2	1' (0)	¾	Flat	None
Ox Creek to Owens Rd.					
	2	1' (0)	¾	Flat	Lock No. 2
Fulton					

USGS (7.5') Maps: Baldwinsville, Pennellville, Fulton, *Lysander.*

The Oswego River has been known to canoeists since the days when Indian paddlers in birchbark canoes travelled this water to Lake Ontario. To the Iroquois, Oswego meant "small water flowing into large;" Ontario meant "a most attractive lake"—and so it still is today.

The river was also known to early French explorers and missionaries such as Samuel de Champlain and Father LeMoyne, and to traders and voyageurs who subsequently came into New York from Canada. Still later, the English and then the Americans knew this waterway as a principal gateway to the west and the expanding continent.

Shortly after Governor Clinton ordered the building of the Erie Canal, work was begun on Oswego Canal, which was dug along the east side of the river from Syracuse to Lake Ontario. With the Oswego Canal's completion, New York City was connected by water to Lake Ontario and all points west.

Although much of what you see on the Oswego today are pleasure boats going to or coming from Lake Ontario, the river is still an important transportation route, serving as part of New York's Barge Canal system which links the St. Lawrence Seaway and Lake Ontario with central New York cities.

In spite of its being broad and slow, the Oswego appeals to canoeists, especially when it is combined with tributaries such as Ox Creek. The Oswego and the Ox are for flatwater paddling (see the chart for low gradients), but that may be just what you want when other nearby streams shrink to a trickle during the summer. Both waterways are wide enough for canoe sailing, while the upper Ox also offers a chance to do some canoe poling. Paddling, sailing, poling—you can put them all together on a single day's outing on the Oswego and the Ox.

There are other attractions as well, such as exploring the backwater sections along the Oswego, or searching for birdlife and waterfowl in Ox Creek swamp, or camping out in an Adirondack lean-to in the Great Bear Cross-Country Skiing and Hiking Area that adjoins the Oswego a short distance downriver from Hinmansville.

Access   Access points are numerous since NY 57 parallels the Oswego for its entire length on the northeast side, and NY 48 does the same on the southwest side.

The suggested take-out spot is at County Route 14 bridge, which crosses the Ox 2 miles west of NY 48. It can be reached by turning west on Wybron Road, located on the south side of Ox Creek near its junction with Oswego River. Drive 1.2 miles to the intersection with County Route 14. Here turn right and continue in a northwest direction for .8 mile to the place where the bridge crosses Ox Creek.

Your put-in is Lock No. 1 in Phoenix. There is a lift bridge that crosses the lock at the corner of State and Culvert Streets. Drive across the bridge and unload your canoe at the north end of the lock. Since the bridge rises to let boats through the lock, it is best to park your vehicle on either State Street or Culvert Street.

Phoenix occupies the site of an old Indian fishing village which was called Kuh-Na-Ta-Ha, and known to the Indians as the "place of the tall pines." It was first visited by Father LeMoyne in 1654. In 1801 Abram Paddock, the first white settler in this region, built a log cabin at your put-in spot.

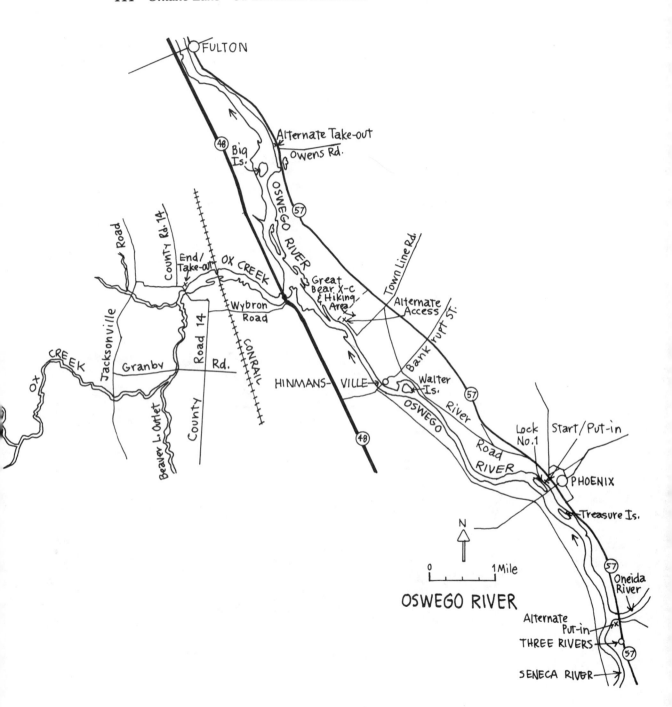

OSWEGO RIVER

The River and Creek The Oswego is one of the big three rivers of central New York. The other two are the Oneida (see Trip 9) and the Seneca (see Trips 10 and 11). It is a large river in width and depth, but short in length—only 19 miles long. It is wide and deep because it is created by the Oneida flowing out of Oneida Lake in the east, and the Seneca flowing out of Seneca Lake in the west. Where these two meet, at a little community appropriately called Three Rivers, the Oswego is formed.

The river drops 120 feet in its short course for a low gradient of 6; dams and control gates have slowed it even more, to make it flatwater the whole way. There are a number of large islands found in the river, such as Treasure Island just south of Phoenix, where French colonists camped when they were escaping from the Onondaga Indians in 1658. In order to lighten their war chest, they deposited a cannon and some gold here—hence, the island's name.

Ox Creek, which has its origin near the hamlet of Lysander 8 miles to the southwest, is a kind of aquatic oddity. For almost 4 miles at its lower end it is as wide as the Oswego itself, making the Ox look more like a river than a creek. Since the water level of the Oswego is controlled to keep it high, the water of the Oswego has pushed up the Ox, swelling it to its present size and making it wide enough for canoe sailing.

Ox Creek looking west.

The Trip
Start/Lock No. 1

Once you're in the water and under way north of Lock No. 1, you have 3 miles of flatwater paddling before your first major landmark, Walter Island. The route is pleasant. Both sides of the river are thickly lined with trees, and even though you can occasionally see houses amid the trees, you are more conscious of green foliage on the banks than of human habitation.

Since the river is wide it will easily display waves and even whitecaps on a windy day, so pick a calm day when there's no headwind for canoeing the Oswego. As soon as you pass Walter Island in either the right or left channel you can see Hinmansville bridge ahead. From the bridge it is about a mile to the recreation site called the Great Bear Cross-Country Skiing and Hiking Area, which is owned and managed by the city of Fulton. A dirt road leads down to, and then along, the river for ¼ mile here. It is a good place to put ashore for lunch. You'll notice several Adirondack-type lean-tos tucked in among the pine trees, as well as other kinds of recreational buildings.

From here it is 1¼ miles to the junction with Ox Creek. You come around a point on your left and paddle a short distance in wide water to a bridge over which NY 48 passes. You're on Ox Creek now, but because of its width it looks like a continuation of the Oswego. The water is clear for a mile upstream, and then the floating weedbeds appear; these are soon replaced by an impressively large stand of arrow arum, but the creek channel, while meandering, is easy to follow.

End/County Route 14 bridge

The Ox narrows as you pass under a railroad bridge, and then widens again. About a mile more through the weed-filled water brings you to the County Route 14 bridge and your take-out spot. But try the Ox above the bridge. Here you'll discover that the channel is wider and deeper than it is in the downstream portion. On all sides are thick tuberous arrow arums, so dense you can't believe there is water stretching more than 1,000 feet across from shore to shore.

This, of course, is a haven for waterfowl—herons and ducks by the score can be seen taking off ahead as you paddle upstream. At the end of a mile the Ox narrows a bit, but if you push on with paddle or pole you can reach South Granby Road bridge ¼ mile upstream. If you're in the mood you can probably canoe another mile on the Ox, but it will be with some difficulty. Pick your turn-around spot anywhere you like, and head back to the bridge. Take out on the northwest side of the bridge; there's a path up the embankment to the road and your waiting vehicle.

Alternate Canoe Routes

You can put in at Three Rivers. This gives you 2¼ miles of paddling past Treasure Island to Phoenix. At the south end of Lock No. 1 is a small park where you can take out, or, if the lockkeeper is accommodating, you can have your canoe locked through.

Upstream there is a nice stretch of water from the junction with Ox Creek to a take-out spot just north of Big Island and on the east side of Owens Road, a distance of 2¼ miles. Of course, if you have the time and inclination, you can paddle down the Oswego from Owens Road to Lake Ontario, a distance of 10 miles with around seven locks.

18

Deer Creek/Lake Ontario

Described Trip:
NY 3 bridge and back
5 miles
Beginner at medium high water

Access Points	Interval Distance	Drop and (Gradient)	Trip Time	Water Conditions	Obstacles
NY 3 bridge					
	½ mile	0' (0)	¼ hour	Flatwater	None
Kelley Road					
	2¼	2' (0)	¾	Flatwater	None
Lake Ontario					

USGS (7.5') Maps: Sandy Creek, Richland, Pulaski.

Head for Deer Creek when you feel like spending a summer day swimming and picnicking on the beach. It is a relatively short paddle—about 3 miles—from the put-in spot to a broad sandy beach on the shore of Lake Ontario. And the paddle back upstream is almost as easy as going down, since the creek has practically no current.

An attractive waterway to canoe, the Deer flows westward through a large 4½-square mile wetland area, Deer Creek Marsh. Even when you're deep in the marsh you can still see trees—ahead, where they line the sandy embankment along Lake Ontario; to the left, covering the high ground that thrusts itself into the marsh like a huge finger; and, for a good share of the trip, on the right as well.

Your destination on the Deer is as pleasing as the sights along the way. The state acquired much of this land in 1978, primarily to protect the wetlands. At that time it was being turned into a trailer-beach area. After the state took over the land, all trailers and outbuildings were cleared. Today only a wide clean beach remains, a mile long, providing access to the waters of Lake Ontario for swimming, and to the soft white sand for sunbathing or beachcombing.

It is a good place to bring fishing gear. There are bass, pickerel and pike in Deer Creek, and, if you are fishing early in the season, you can take from 5 to 10-pound brown trout near the shore in Lake Ontario.

Deer Creek Marsh is also a bird sanctuary, a choice place for the bird watcher looking for shore birds and waterfowl.

Access

Deer Creek is on the east shore of Lake Ontario, about half way between Syracuse and Watertown. It can be easily reached via NY 3. Take NY 13 west from Pulaski (just off I-81), and drive 3.2 miles to its intersection with NY 3 at Port Ontario. Turn right onto NY 3 and drive north over the bridge that crosses the Salmon River. Two miles beyond that bridge, NY 3 crosses Deer Creek.

Park on the right side of the highway, well off the road. This is a two-lane route, heavily used by vacationers. The embankment leading to the river is a bit steep, but it isn't too hard to get a canoe down and into the water.

The Creek

Like several of its nearby cousins that empty into the eastern end of Lake Ontario, Deer Creek has its origin in the foothills of Tug Hill—fifteen miles away in the town of Boylston, about a mile and a half west of the hamlet of Smartville.

There the elevation is 950 feet, giving the Deer a drop of 700 feet by the time it reaches Lake Ontario, for an impressive gradient of 48. However, the upper section of the Deer is not canoeable, and so this gradient has no practical importance for the paddler. The lower section of the creek is flat, with virtually no gradient at all.

Just before the brook-sized Deer Creek reaches NY 3 it is joined by Little Deer Creek which flows in from the south. This stream follows a route parallel to Deer Creek's, except that Little Deer starts only seven-and-a-half miles away. When these two streams combine their resources a broad, canoeable waterway suddenly materializes.

As it moves through Deer Creek Marsh the Deer becomes respectably wide and deep. About ½ mile from its end, the creek butts against the narrow but high land strip of sand that separates the marsh from Lake Ontario, forcing it to

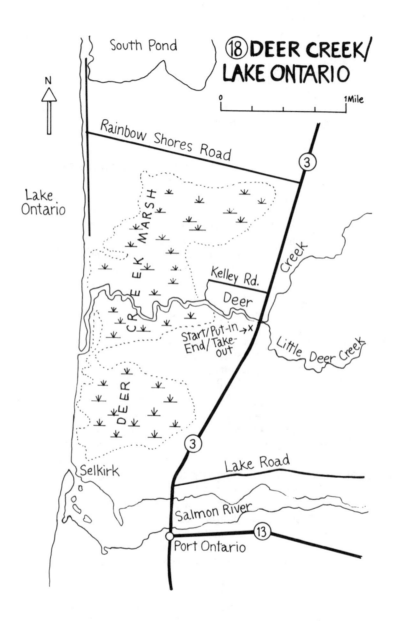

⑱ DEER CREEK/ LAKE ONTARIO

South Pond

N

Lake Ontario

Rainbow Shores Road

3

CREEK MARSH

Kelley Rd.

Creek

Deer

Start/Put-in →x
End/Take-out

Little Deer Creek

DEER

3

Selkirk

Lake Road

Salmon River

13

Port Ontario

0   1Mile

Where the Deer Creek meets Lake Ontario.

flow south, parallel to the land strip, before emptying into the lake.

The Trip
Start/NY 3 bridge

This is a round trip that starts and ends at NY 3, after a float to Lake Ontario and a leisurely paddle back upstream.

Put in at the northwest side of the NY 3 bridge; that gives you the easiest access to the creek. Once you are in the water and heading downstream the open fields surrounding you rapidly give way to tall trees that line the banks. About ½ mile farther downstream the trees recede. At the mile mark you are well into Deer Creek Marsh.

About a mile wide and 3 miles long, this wetland area runs from Selkirk at the mouth of the Salmon River in the south, to South Pond in the north. Deer Creek is the marsh's sole drainage route to Lake Ontario.

Waterfowl, especially evident during the spring mating season, appear as you move into the marsh. The Deer begins to snake about in a series of small and then larger loops as it makes its way through the wetland.

At the 1½ mile point a few small bends in the creek bring you to the high dunes. Less than 100 yards beyond is Lake Ontario. On days when west winds are blowing across the lake you can hear waves breaking on the beach.

The landscape changes abruptly as the Deer makes an elbow turn to the south. The marsh environment is gone, and in its place is high land, covered with trees and rising at least 40 feet from the water's edge. Deer Creek appears to be flowing through a deep channel. A half mile downstream the creek broadens and becomes surprisingly shallow. You are encountering a delta, where the stream deposits its sediment.

Take a turn to the right. Before you is the vast openness of Lake Ontario, with sandy beaches stretching to the left and right. On the left is private land and a trailer park used primarily by summer vacationists. The state-owned land lies to the right.

End/NY 3 bridge

After you have enjoyed the beach you can return to your canoe and head back upstream. If you keep a sharp eye, you may see waterfowl and other birdlife that you missed on your way down. An hour of paddling brings you back to the NY 3 bridge and your take-out point.

Alternate Canoe Routes

Instead of putting in at NY 3, canoeists in a hurry to get to the beach can drive down Kelley Road .7 mile, and launch their canoes where that road meets the creek. This move reduces the distance to Lake Ontario by ½ mile.

19

Salmon River/Salmon River Reservoir

Described Trip:
Ryan Road to Pineville bridge
11½ miles
Intermediate at medium water
Advanced and expert at medium and high water

Access Points	Interval Distance	Drop and (Gradient)	Trip Time	Water Conditions	Obstacles
Osceola					
	2½ miles	98' (41)		Fastwater, whitewater	Dead trees
Ryan Road bridge					
	2½	*4' (2)*	1 hr.	*Flatwater, fastwater*	*None*
Waterbury Road bridge					
	2	4' (2)			Posted waters, no canoeing allowed
Salmon River Reservoir, east end					
	6	*4' (0)*	2½	*Stillwater*	*None*
Salmon River Reservoir, west end					
	3	282' (94)		Not canoeable	Little water, falls
Lower Reservoir, east end					
	¾	4' (0)		Stillwater	None
Lower Reservoir, west end					
	2	131' (72)		Fastwater	Water release, boulders, chutes
Altmar					
	3¼	*25' (8)*	1¼	*Fastwater, flatwater*	*Water release*
Pineville					
	6¼	129' (21)		Fastwater, whitewater	Water release, rocks
Pulaski					
	3½	101' (28)		Whitewater, fastwater	Water release, rocks, boulders
Port Ontario					
	1½	15' (10)		Flatwater	None
Selkirk (Lake Ontario)					

USGS (7.5') Maps: High Market, Point Rock, East Florence, North Osceola, Redfield, Orwell, Richland, *Pulaski.*

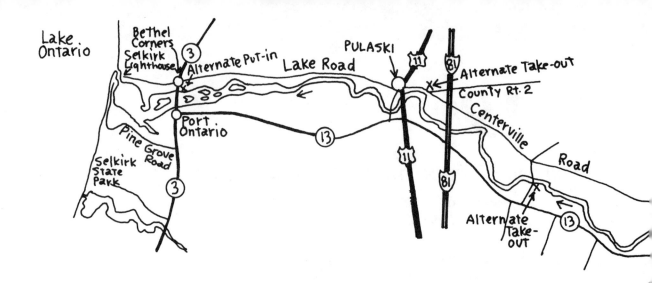

At times the Salmon can be a tumbling, churning, terrifying river; at other times it can be completely calm. In places it becomes a long, broad, island-dotted lake; in others, reduced to a trickle, it virtually disappears.

Man and nature have combined to provide for the canoeist an extraordinary mixture of conditions here, ranging from the turbulent to the tranquil, the wild to the civilized, and the unexpected to the commonplace.

Since only half of the Salmon's 48 miles are canoeable, it is all the more remarkable to find this river offering such variety. Some credit goes to the Niagara Mohawk Power Corporation's engineers who dammed the middle section of the river in two places, producing the large, 6-mile-long Salmon River Reservoir which runs west of Redfield, and the smaller, ¾-mile-long Lower Reservoir at Bennett Bridge.

Nature gets the credit for other spectacular aspects of the Salmon. The river flows from its source high in the Tug Hill region, down flinty slopes, emptying finally into Lake Ontario, for a drop of 1,570 feet and a substantial gradient of 32.

So who can canoe the Salmon? The answer is that anyone can—novice or expert, canoeist or kayaker, paddler or sailor. The river favors all; you've just got to know where to put in and where to take out.

It is not a river you can canoe from one end to the other. The Salmon is chopped up and divided by dams and posted signs; so one must plan for long-distance carries.

It is also important on the Salmon to plan for the possibility of suddenly rising or falling water. Water is released from the dams to generate power, and during these water-release periods (usually in the morning on weekdays) the river can rise as much as two feet, turning a flatwater section into a whitewater stretch.

In late summer these releases are welcome, since they can make routes such as the one from Altmar to Pineville bridge a fast, exciting stretch to canoe.

SALMON RIVER/SALMON RESERVOIR

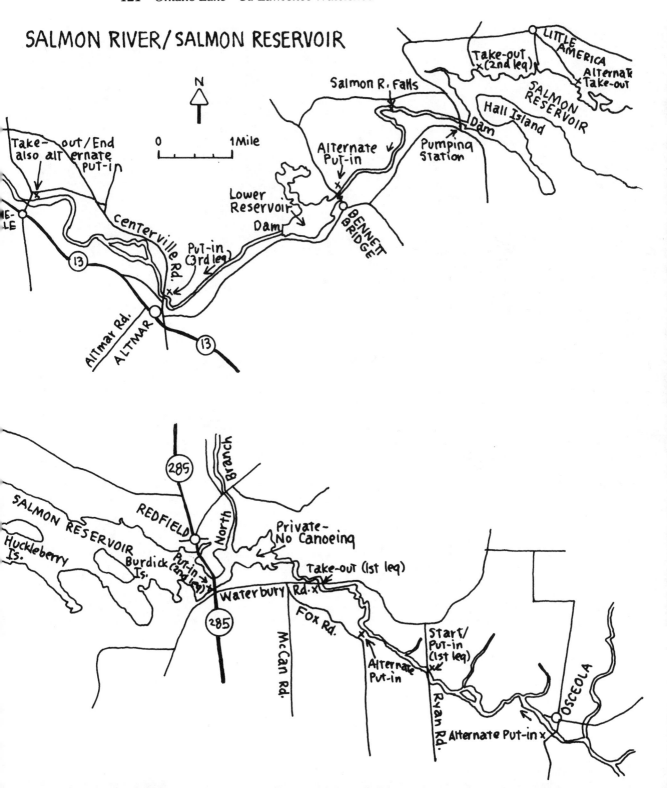

Rapids on the Salmon River.

However, after a rain or when the water is high with the spring runoff, an increase in the water level and velocity can catch the uninformed by surprise and even result in tragedy. But information is available. Niagara Mohawk operates a hot line for fishermen and canoeists. Just call 315-298-6531. A recorded announcement will tell you when the water will be released and the time and places it will rise.

Access

For a day's outing, we recommend a series of three routes: from Ryan Road bridge to Waterbury Road bridge in the upper section, from the east end to the northwest end of the main reservoir, and from Altmar to Pineville in the middle section.

You'll have no difficulty reaching the various access points along the river and at the reservoirs. The take-out spot for the first leg of your trip is at Waterbury Road bridge, 2½ miles downstream from your put-in point. (Below Waterbury Road bridge for 2 miles to the reservoir itself the land and the river are posted by a private club in Redfield.) To get to this first take-out spot, follow County Route 2 east out of Pulaski to Redfield, where you turn south. Cross the bridge at the east end of the reservoir to intersect Waterbury Road. Turn left on Waterbury Road and drive 1.6 miles to where it crosses the Salmon River. This is the take-out spot.

To get to the put-in point, continue east on Waterbury Road for another 1.5 miles to Ryan Road; drive south on this road .5 mile to the bridge crossing the Salmon. Park here and launch your canoe.

On the reservoir itself your take-out spot is found at the northwest end; here at the end of Jackson Road is a launching site as well as good-sized parking area for vehicles. The put-in spot is situated at a boat launching site where the reservoir begins immediately west of the NY 285 bridge a short distance south of Redfield.

In the middle section, your take-out spot is on the northeast side of the Pineville bridge; here adjoining the river, you will find a fishing access site and parking lot. Your put-in spot is the bridge crossing the Salmon on the northern edge of Altmar.

The River

The Salmon is one of the most popular racing streams in central New York. The section from Altmar to Pulaski is a particular favorite for serious canoe and kayak racing, including national competitions sanctioned by the American Canoe Association.

It is also one of New York's finest trout and salmon streams. Brook trout are found in the upper section, but in the lower section from Lake Ontario to Altmar are found the giants—coho and Chinook salmon, steelheads, and brown trout, many weighing over twenty pounds. For decades the river's namesake was missing from these waters, but in the 1960's state aquatic biologists successfully reintroduced several species of salmon, as well as the rainbows and browns. Today the river attracts fishermen from all over the nation.

The headwaters of the Salmon begin high in the Tug Hill region and deep in the Lesser Wilderness area where there are no roads, only a vast hardwood forest. The water flows south, and then arcs west to pass its first point of civilization, the hamlet of Osceola, where it is joined by Fall Brook. From here the river flows westward into the main reservoir. An aqueduct runs water from the dam to the Lower Reservoir, reducing the river to a trickle. Below the lower dam, however, the Salmon becomes itself again, rushing past Altmar, then widening and slowing as it approaches Pineville. From here past Pulaski the river picks up speed, becoming fastwater and, at high levels, whitewater. In the lower end the river widens and slows dramatically for about 1 ½ miles before it serenely enters Lake Ontario.

The Trip
Start/Ryan Road bridge

At your put-in point the river is narrow but canoeable well into summer. The area is open at first, but you soon move into the state forest. As you approach Waterbury Road the river begins to turn and twist, straightening as you reach your take-out point by the bridge.

Haul your canoe down to your put-in point at the east end of the reservoir. You can now have a leisurely cruise down the reservoir, providing you are not bucking a headwind out of the west. Birdlife, including ducks and herons, is abundant here if you explore the various inlets and coves. You may also like exploring the islands, such as the larger Burdick and Huckleberry Islands, or the many smaller ones, which many canoeists think are especially interesting.

Take out at the Jackson Road launch site at the northwest end of the reservoir and shuttle your canoe to Altmar. If you have time you may wish to paddle the Lower Reservoir and adjoining ponds. In Altmar, find the bridge that crosses the river and put in there.

The trip downstream should be a leisurely one at low water, but it will be fast at high water after a release from the dam. About ½ mile below Altmar the river splits into three streams for nearly a mile before coming together again. Follow the right channel.

End/Pineville bridge

The river is now flowing through a narrow, forested valley with the land high on both sides. It runs through several slow turns, past the first cluster of small islands, then follows a straight route to another set of four larger islands just before reaching your take-out point at Pineville bridge. For those eager to do more paddling there is a 3-mile run from the Pineville bridge to a lower bridge downriver. The water here is fairly fast at low water, and challenging at high water.

Alternate Canoe Routes

The Salmon with its two reservoirs offers a number of possible canoe routes. The 6-mile-long main reservoir can, of course, be paddled as a single body of water; and you can easily spend all day on the reservoir exploring the inlets, coves, and islands. Exploring the Lower Reservoir and the water routes leading to several nearby ponds is also worthwhile.

To get a good taste of fastwater canoeing, wait for water release time. When the water comes up, try the 6¼-mile section from Pineville bridge to Pulaski; take out at the western edge of the village, where you will find a large parking area a short distance east of the fish weir. You'll encounter low rapids and chutes as well as numerous fast runs en route; hence, this section at high water is for intermediate or advanced canoeists.

The two-mile section below Pulaski is the whitewater stretch and should be run only by advanced or expert canoeists. The mile-long stretch at the bottom to Port Ontario is flatwater and can be paddled by novices.

20

South Sandy Creek/Lakeview Pond

Described Trip:
Lakeview Pond to NY 3 bridge
12 miles
Novice at low and medium water

Access Points	Interval Distance	Drop and (Gradient)	Trip Time	Water Conditions	Obstacles
SOUTH SANDY CREEK					
Ellisburg					
	3½ miles	40' (10)	2 hours	Flatwater, riffles	None
NY 3 Bridge					
	2	5' (3)	1	Flatwater	None
Lake Ontario					
NORTH SANDY CREEK					
US 11 Bridge					
	2	70' (36)	1	Fastwater, rapids	Falls
Wardwell Settlement Road Bridge					
	3	218' (73)	1	Fastwater	Falls
NY 3 Bridge					
	2½	22' (8)	1½	Flatwater	None
Lake Ontario					
LAKEVIEW POND OUTLET					
Boat Launch Site					
	2	5' (3)	1	Flatwater	None
Jct. North Sandy					
	1	1' (1)	½	Flatwater	None
Lake Ontario					

USGS (7.5') Maps: Rodman, Adams, Ellisburg, Sandy Creek, *Henderson.*

Here a vast wetland region encompasses a network of interconnected ponds, streams, and channels, all flowing into Lake Ontario—as fine an area for family canoeing as you'll find in central New York.

Known as the state's Lakeview Wildlife Management Area, the region offers something for everyone: backwater paddling, spring quickwater runs, creek cruising, canoe sailing, canoe poling, excellent birding, exciting fishing, and exploring, with some nice spots for picnicking and swimming thrown in.

As you move westward toward Lake Ontario, you find habitat usually associated with wetlands and backwater: tall marsh grass and cattails, arrow arum, pickerelweed, water hyacinth, and pond lilies. As you move upstream away from the lake the land rises, and soon you are surrounded by farmland, with hardwoods lining the creek edges.

Not surprisingly, this is a nesting and resting area for many different birds and waterfowl. In the late spring and early fall, the broad sandy beaches of Lake Ontario are stopping places for a wide variety of migrating shore birds. Both puddle ducks and diving ducks are found here by the hundreds, and during migration periods their numbers swell into the thousands.

Fishing is of the bragging sort. In early summer smallmouth bass are caught in great numbers. During the summer great northern pike ranging up to fifteen pounds cruise the inland waterways. Then there are Lake Ontario's big trout: browns, rainbows (or steelheads). Chinook salmon range from three to eight pounds, and cohoes run as large as fifteen pounds. Both trout and salmon can be found in the upstream waters during their spring or fall spawning runs.

Access
The canoeable area lies along the east shore of Lake Ontario, immediately south of Southwick Beach State Park, a fine place for overnight camping and daytime recreation. Originating in the Tug Hill region, the waters of both North Sandy and South Sandy Creeks flow westward into Lake Ontario, and are part of the St. Lawrence-Lake Ontario North Flow watershed.

The area can be reached by I-81 via Ellisburg, or NY 3 via Pulaski, with the latter route the recommended one. From Pulaski NY 13 takes you west to Port Ontario and the intersection with NY 3. Drive north on NY 3 for 11 miles through Sandy Ponds Corners to the bridge crossing South Sandy Creek. This is a good take-out point if you are not planning to make a round trip back to your launching site. You can turn left off NY 3 to the boat launch area and parking lot, and leave vehicles here for the pickup and shuttle run back.

Continue north on NY 3 for another three miles to Lakeview Road, which intersects from the left. Turn onto Lakeview Road and drive .5 mile to its dead end at Lakeview Pond. You are now on state land. Here you will find a convenient boat launch site and a parking lot. The area is shaded by large trees, making it a nice spot for a picnic.

The Creeks and Ponds
The marsh extends west from NY 3 to the shores of Lake Ontario, 4 miles long, and 1½ miles wide at its widest point. In the northern portion is ¾-mile-long Lakeview Pond, which drains via a narrow channel south to Sandy Creek (known popularly as North Sandy Creek). This, in turn, flows into Floodwood Pond. From Floodwood the water flows a short distance to empty into Lake Ontario.

The waters of South Sandy Creek come from the south to meet those draining

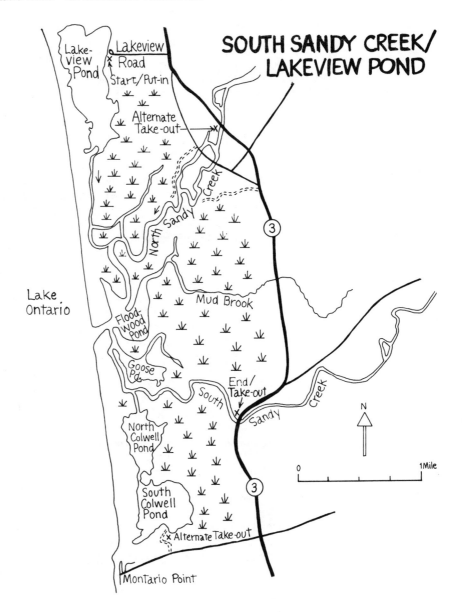

SOUTH SANDY CREEK/ LAKEVIEW POND

from Goose Pond; together they join the water flowing from Floodwood Pond. When the water is sufficiently high there is a channel connecting South Sandy with two interconnected ponds in the southern portion of the Lakeview Wildlife Management Area—North Colwell Pond, and its slightly larger sister, South Colwell Pond. A dirt road running from the Montario Point paved road reaches the south shore of South Colwell Pond, where there is a parking area and a boat launch.

Lake Ontario is separated from the marsh area by a narrow but long natural barrier of sand dunes topped by tall trees: aspen, birch, pine, ash, and maple. Lakeview Pond is situated immediately east of the dunes.

The Trip
Start/Lakeview Pond

Once you have put in at Lakeview Pond boat launch, paddle to the far side of the pond, climb the sand dune, and walk down onto the handsome shore of Lake Ontario. You are now on the state-owned, "forever wild" beach, which runs four miles south of Southwick Beach State Park. No picnicking, camping, or swimming are permitted along this stretch of beach. Only walking and looking are allowed.

Continue south on Lakeview Pond. Soon it narrows into a deep channel which runs ⅔ of a mile in a straight line, parallel to the sand dunes that rise on your right. By this time you have begun to see waterfowl, perhaps a blue heron or two. Follow the main channel until it turns left and enters the wider waterway of North Sandy. The water is still deep and slow moving. Another ⅔ of a mile will bring you to Floodwood Pond.

But before going on to the pond, canoeing North Sandy is worth the required time and energy. You may wish to go only part of the way to the NY 3 bridge, which is just short of two miles upstream. The first mile up the creek is marshland; then trees begin to appear, providing a picturesque setting. At the mile-and-a-half mark a few houses on your right and several more farther upstream will remind you that you are moving from state to private land.

Back at Floodwater Pond you can do some exploring by paddling up to where it narrows and receives water from Mud Brook, or you can continue following the current to the pond's mouth and Lake Ontario. Here again you can put ashore and enjoy walking the lake's wide beaches. When ready, proceed southward, upcurrent, into South Sandy Creek. If you feel like more exploring, Goose Pond lies off to your left.

The next two miles take you up South Sandy as it snakes eastward through the marsh, flowing deep and slow. Paddling upstream is easy; you are hardly aware of a current. After you have been on South Sandy for a half mile see if you can find the channel to the Colwell Ponds. If you do find it you can add these ponds to your trip.

End/NY 3 bridge

Trees begin to appear along the banks as you approach NY 3. Soon the creek edges are densely lined with trees and other high ground vegetation. Ahead is the NY 3 bridge and your take-out point. However, you should continue upstream for at least another mile. It is an attractive stretch with trees forming a canopy over the stream, providing shade on a hot day. During late spring and early summer you can advance quite a distance up South Sandy, but in midsummer the water becomes shallow and the trip scratchy beyond the mile mark. Now reverse direction and take out at the bridge.

Alternate Canoe Routes

Given the several access points, there are a number of different routes that can be followed. A popular alternative to the described trip is to put-in and take-out at Lakeview Pond, paddling down to Lake Ontario, up South Sandy until your canoe scrapes bottom a half mile or so east of the NY 3 bridge, then returning to your starting place. Another is to canoe south from Lakeview Pond, take in the lower sections of North and South Sandy, and end on the Colwell Ponds with a take-out on the south shore of South Colwell Pond. It is also possible to take-out where the NY 3 bridge crosses North Sandy.

*Mohawk Watershed
(East Flow)*

21

Black Creek/Hinckley Reservoir

Described Trip:
NY 8 bridge to Hinckley Reservoir
Beach and Picnic Area
9¼ miles
Novice at medium high water
Intermediate at high water

Access Points	Interval Distance	Drop and (Gradient)	Trip Time	Water Conditions	Obstacles
Bridge next to Santmire Road					
	2 miles	3' (1)	¾ hour	Flat, riffles	None
NY 8 bridge					
	1¾	0' (0)	¾	Flat	None
Fisher Road bridge					
	4	2' (½)	1¼	Flat	None
Black Creek Road bridge					
	2½	5' (4)	1	Flat, riffles	None
Grant Road bridge (Grant)					
	½	3' (2)	¼	Flat	None
Jct. Hinckley Reservoir					
	½	0' (0)	¼	Flat	None
Hinckley Reservoir Beach & Picnic Area					

USGS (15') Map: Ohio, *USGS (7.5') Map:* Hinckley.

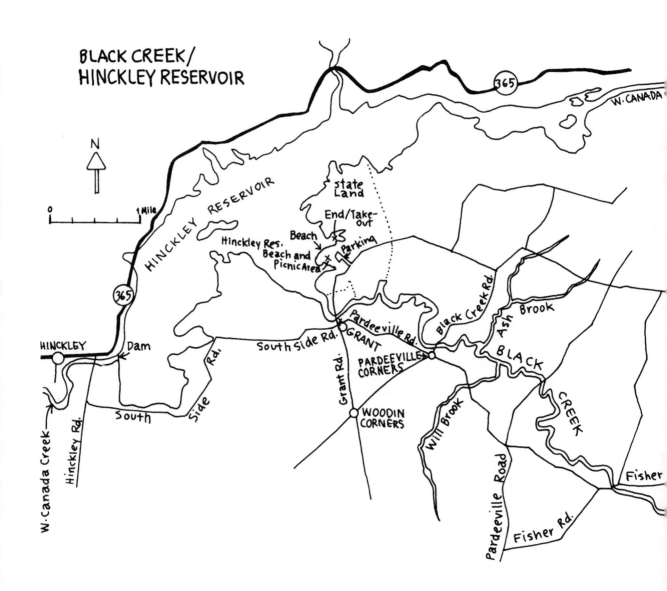

BLACK CREEK/
HINCKLEY RESERVOIR

Think of Black Creek as a boundary that marks the end of the Adirondacks and the beginning of central New York. This 27-mile-long stream lies between Adirondack foothills on the north and flatlands to the south, between thick northern forest lands and southern farmlands, between wilderness and civilization. To canoe Black Creek is to get a mix of two worlds.

Black Creek also offers two worlds of canoeing—creek cruising and lake sailing, with sizable Hinckley Reservoir providing conditions for the latter sport. Hinckley is 7 miles long and 1½ miles across, giving you—if you're lucky enough to have good wind—plenty of room for a full day of fast canoe sailing.

The Black, like Ninemile Creek (see Trip 23), has something of an identity problem. Several streams in central New York are called "Black." Because of their close proximity, Black Creek is especially easy to confuse with Black River, its wider and more robust cousin a mere 4 miles to the north.

So, when talking about Black Creek, you need to mention that it is 16 miles north of Utica, and that it flows northwest into Hinckley Reservoir (which on some maps is also called Kuyahoora Lake). That should take care of location and identification problems.

For many canoeists Black Creek is appealing because it is unpretentious and, outside of its own environs, almost unknown. The creek goes about its business in such a matter-of-fact manner that its unusual features are often overlooked, such as its ability to flow northward to reach the south. (Study the terrain to figure that one out.) And sometimes this creek may be deeper and wider in its middle section than in its lower stretches, particularly when the reservoir is low.

It flows through regions that sound as though the creek were in Europe. First come the towns of Stratford and Salisbury. They adjoin the town of Norway. Next come Russia and Poland, and then Holland Patent. And to add to the variety (to say nothing of the confusion when you try to tell people where you've been), there is Ohio (the town) and Ohio (the hamlet), Trenton, Newport, California Clearing, and California Trail.

Waiting at the end of your cruise is the state-operated Hinckley Reservoir Beach and Picnic Area. There is an entrance fee. The beach is broad and sandy, and on a hot summer day a refreshing swim here is a fine way to finish your trip.

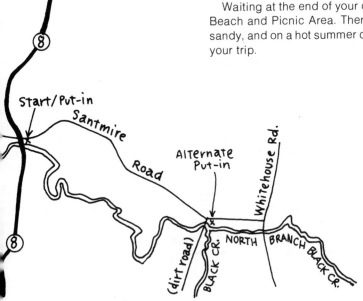

Access   Coming from the west, the most direct route to Black Creek is via NY 365, which can be found a few miles east of Rome. NY 365 brings you to the hamlet of Hinckley, which sits to one side of the reservoir dam. Coming from Utica (in the south), take NY 12 and then NY 365. From Herkimer, take NY 28 and then NY 365.

The suggested take-out is Hinckley Reservoir Beach and Picnic Area on the reservoir's southeast side. To get there, in the hamlet of Hinckley turn off NY 365 onto Hinckley Road. Drive ½ mile south, then bear left onto South Side Road, and follow it for 3.2 miles to Grant Road. Turn left here, and .7 mile brings you to the Area's entrance. An alternate take-out that shortens your trip by a mile is found at the Grant Road bridge.

The put-in spot is at the NY 8 bridge, 7.3 miles north of the village of Poland. Santmire Road intersects from the east; vehicles can be parked along the edge of this road. Launch your canoe on the northeast corner of the bridge.

The Creek and Reservoir   The first half of Black is a wilderness stream in the wildest section of the southern Adirondacks where there are no cabins, no human beings, and no roads—not even a foot trail. To get to the Black's source at Black Creek Lake would require a bushwhacking expedition that few would attempt and fewer could accomplish. The Black's lower section, on the other hand, passes through civilized country, flowing under paved highway bridges, past roads, farms, and pastureland.

The creek starts its career on the run, racing, tumbling, and even snarling its way down a long slope to the flatland that begins at the hamlet of Gray, for a drop of 830 feet. From here to the Hinckley Reservoir, however, Black Creek alters its demeanor, with a drop of only 50 feet for a relatively flat gradient of 5.

The Black gathers its water from a region that's filled with the use of the word "vly"—a word of Dutch origin, meaning low marshy area: Vly Creek, Comstock Vly, Twin Vlys, Little York Vly, Thorp Vly, Crosby Vly, and Hall Vly. In its lower section the Black holds onto this water well into the summer, to make it a respectably canoeable stream even in August.

In its upper reaches the Black flows an almost straight westerly course. At Gray, however, it turns in a more northerly direction as it heads for what was at one time Kuyahoora Lake. Today the lake has been replaced by the larger Hinckley Reservoir, which is dammed at its west end for electric power-generating purposes. The main source of the reservoir's water is West Canada Creek (see Trip 22), which starts far to the north in the Adirondack heartland. Water released from the reservoir continues as the West Canada in a southward course past Poland, Newport, and Middleville, finally emptying into the Mohawk River at Herkimer. By emptying into the reservoir, Black Creek becomes a tributary of West Canada Creek, and part of the Mohawk River watershed.

The Trip
Start/NY 8 bridge   Once you have your canoe in the water at the NY 8 bridge, paddle west under the bridge. A short distance beyond, Black Creek bends to the left, only to turn back again to its westward course. A couple more small bends and about a mile of paddling brings you to Fisher Road bridge. Along this route thick vegetation—mostly alder—overhangs the creek edge.

A wilderness-like stretch of Black Creek.

Below Fisher Road bridge, a mixed stand of evergreen and hardwood appear on the shoreline, even though the land on both sides of the creek is flat open terrain. But about ½ mile downstream the ecology changes; the fields give way to thick woods, much of it evergreen.

In the 4-mile stretch between Fisher Road bridge and Black Creek Road bridge at Pardeeville Corners, the creek does a lot of wiggling, snaking back and forth and, in several places, almost forming oxbows. The water here is flat and slow-moving. Below Black Creek Road bridge, however, the creek drops a bit, causing a short run of riffles and, when the water is on the low side, producing a certain amount of scratchiness.

The riffle section soon gives way to a much deeper and wider stretch of creek which looks like an Adirondack stream, flanked on both sides with tall stands of pine mixed with maple. The creek now heads due north for a short distance, and then swings west. After a wiggle or two it turns in a more southerly direction for the next ¾ mile to the hamlet of Grant.

The water level above and below Grant Road bridge varies with the water level in the reservoir. Since the reservoir's water is used to generate power, its level drops gradually during the summer months, and, of course, so does the creek's level. When the reservoir is full, the creek's level may be up 10 to 17 feet above its lowest level in late summer. If you are looking for high water, it is best to check the creek's level before starting your trip.

End/Hinckley Reservoir Beach and Picnic Area

A half mile beyond Grant Road bridge brings you to the junction with Hinckley Reservoir. Follow the reservoir's shoreline northward for ½ mile. Paddle beyond the beach and into the neck of a small brook outlet. Take out here and carry back to your waiting vehicle.

Alternate Canoe Routes

Hinckley Reservoir offers a lot of water and more shoreline than can be followed in a day's paddle. There are numerous inlets and several feeder streams that are fun to explore, as well as an island about a mile west of Black Creek's entrance.

Other canoeing options are a little more distant. You can put in at or below Trenton Falls (see Trip 22) for a trip on the lower half of West Canada Creek; or you can travel north on NY 8 to either Morehouseville or Hoffmeister, and take a dirt road north a short distance to put in on the South Branch of West Canada Creek.

22

West Canada Creek

Described Trip:
Partridge Hill Road to
Fishing access site on NY 28
11¼ miles
Novice at low water
Intermediate to advanced on high water

Access Points	Interval Distance	Drop and (Gradient)	Trip Time	Water Conditions	Obstacles
Trenton Falls					
	1½ miles	10' (7)	½ hrs.	Fast, low rapids	None
Partridge Hill Road Put-in Site					
	1¼	5' (4)	½	*Fast, low rapids, riffles*	*Some rocks*
Jct. Cincinnati Ck.					
	1½	5' (3)	½	Moderate, riffles	Some rocks
1st NY 28 bridge/parking area					
	1¼	30' (24)	⅓	Fast, rapids, chutes	None
2nd NY 28 bridge					
	3¼	20' (6)	1	Moderate, low rapids, runs	None
NY 8/28 bridge					
	1½	20' (13)	½	Moderate, low rapids, riffles	Some rocks
Old State Rd. bridge (Poland)					
	1	10' (10)	¼	Moderate, riffles, runs	None
Fishing Access/ parking area					
	4	40' (10)	1½	Fast, rapids, chutes	Rock gardens
Newport dam & bridge					
	7	60' (9)	2	Fast, rapids, chutes	Some boulders
Middleville					
	6½	40' (6)	2	Fast, rapids, riffles, runs	Some rocks
Kast Bridge					
	3¼	40' (12)	1	Fast, rapids, chutes	Some rocks
NY 28 bridge (Herkimer)					
	1	20' (20)	¼	Fast, rapids	None
Jct. Mohawk River					

USGS (7.5') Maps: Rensen, South Trenton, Newport, *Middleville, Herkimer.*

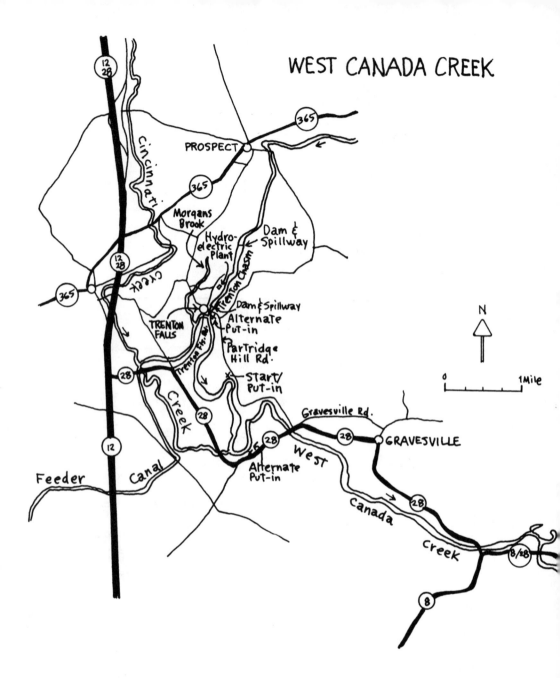

WEST CANADA CREEK

Trout fishermen and canoe paddlers tend to look at water from different perspectives and with different expectations. But when they describe West Canada Creek, members of both parties use the same word—the creek's "beautiful"!

They mean beautiful in all respects: the water, the setting, the scenery, and variety. But the water is most important. It's clear, clean, and fast-moving

—qualities which both fishermen and paddlers prize.

These are the factors that make West Canada one of New York's top trout streams. Flycasters and spincasters can be found scattered all along the creek's length, testing their lures, techniques, and hopes on the finny inhabitants. In the upper reaches you find the handsome brook trout, and in the lower section you find the wily brown.

Clearwater and fastwater are also the ingredients of a fine canoe stream, and West Canada has them and more. Actually, it is two waterways—a high water stream and a low water stream. The high water version of West Canada comes into existence for several hours every day, when water to generate hydroelectric power is released north of Trenton Falls.

With such releases, West Canada rises quickly from 1½ to 2 feet. This, of course, is when West Canada is at its canoeable best; pools and riffles are replaced by fast, deep runs. In general the rocky sections become well covered with water.

When the dam gates are closed West Canada returns to its low water state. Fishermen now appear in their hip boots and waders, searching out trout pools. Most of West Canada is still canoeable during the low periods, but there are sections—such as the stretch between Poland and Newport—which become scratchy, and hang-ups and canoe dragging are common.

The people who named New York's waterways weren't overly concerned with the distinction between "river" and "creek." We have streams such as Sangerfield River (see Trip 2) which have all the attributes of nice creeks, while West Canada, with all the classic characteristics of a river, is called a creek. When you hear West Canada, think *river.*

Equally baffling is the origin of the name "West Canada." In part the answer is found in the creek's source—a cluster of lakes deep in the central Adirondacks, collectively called West Canada Lakes. But they aren't even near Canada, much less near Canada's West.

However, it isn't names that make good rivers; water, gradient, and scenery do. West Canada has the right amounts and combinations of each, making it one of the most exciting streams to canoe in central New York.

Access   West Canada can easily be reached by taking either NY 12 or NY 8 north from Utica, or NY 28 north from Herkimer. NY 28 follows the creek from a point just below Trenton Falls south to Herkimer, a few miles north of the place where West Canada empties into the Mohawk River.

For the suggested trip the take-out spot is 1½ miles southeast of Poland, at a

Getting ready to shove off on West Canada.

public fishing access site and parking area which the state has constructed next to the stream and NY 28.

The put-in spot lies to the northwest. From the public fishing access site, drive 6½ miles north on NY 28 through Poland toward Trenton. Just before you reach your third bridge crossing West Canada, a road intersects on the right. Turn here. The road immediately forks into Partridge Hill Road and Gravesville Road. Bear to your left and follow Partridge Hill Road (which is now a dirt road) for 1.4 miles. This brings you to a spot on your left where the road and stream are closest. A short carry along a path through some trees takes you to the creek's edge and your launching site.

An alternate put-in spot is located a mile north on Partridge Hill Road on the southeast side of the Trenton Falls bridge.

The Creek With a length of 76 miles, West Canada is one of New York's longer streams. It begins its career at the water outflow of two interconnected lakes, South Lake and Mud Lake, which together with West Lake make up the West Canada Lakes in the central Adirondack region at an elevation of 2,345 feet.

The creek flows southwest into the impoundment called Hinckley Reservoir (formerly known as Kuyahoora Lake), and then out of the reservoir's south end, past Prospect, to a dam where the water releases are controlled.

The release times vary, depending on the amount of water in Hinckley Reservoir (which is administered by the state). Generally, water is released at 8 A.M. Monday through Friday, and at 8 P.M. on weekends. To get the release times, call Niagara Mohawk Power Corporation's Harbor Point, Utica office: 315-732-2111, Ext. 361.

Below Prospect, West Canada races for a mile through a deep, awesome gorge, Trenton Chasm, to reach another, smaller dam on the north side of Trenton Falls bridge at the hamlet of Trenton Falls. West Canada begins now to bend its course to the southwest as it rushes past Poland, Middleville, Kast Bridge, and Herkimer, finally joining the east-flowing Mohawk on the southeast side of Herkimer at an elevation of 308 feet.

From beginning to end West Canada drops 2,037 feet for an impressive gradient of 27, which gives you an idea of the stream's lively character. In the suggested 11¼-mile stretch from the Partridge Hill Road put-in to the take-out south of Poland, the drop is a little short of 100 feet for a gradient of 9—just steep enough to keep the water flow in the fast class at low water.

When the gates are opened at the dam, however, things quickly change along this route. The creek rises several feet and speeds up considerably to about 5 miles per hour; runs become longer and faster, and the riffle and low rapid sections change to stretches of higher rapids and chutes.

The landscape is rural and attractive; the creek is tree-lined for its entire distance. The stretch from Trenton Falls to the take-out spot at the public fishing access site can be canoed when the water is low during most of the summer.

The section farther south to Newport, on the other hand, is thinner, producing hang-ups. It also is a section that is filled with rocks and boulders. At low water it can be canoed, with a certain amount of dragging. At high water this section is tricky, indeed, for just below the water's surface are the boulders' tops. Avoiding these requires swift maneuvering.

The Trip   At high water West Canada moves briskly past the launching site, but it is not difficult to get under way. There are some boulders in this section, but generally they are well above or well below the water's surface. The trip described here is a high water one; hence, paddlers ought to be in the intermediate class, experienced in river hydraulics and in running rapids and chutes.

Start/Partridge Hill Road   From the put-in point, the creek races due south for ½ mile where it splits around a good-sized island; stay to the right. Another ¼ mile downstream West Canada takes in water from Cincinnati Creek, a stream which can be canoed in spring and early summer from Remsen to the junction with West Canada.

West Canada now begins to loop back onto itself, almost forming an oxbow. En route you pass over several swift runs with foot-high standing waves. As West Canada loops northward, however, the stream widens and flattens somewhat, and the current runs steady. A mile downstream West Canada again loops, this time bending to the right and heading in a southeasterly direction. A half mile brings you to the first NY 28 bridge.

Below the bridge West Canada bears in a more easterly direction; the scenery here is attractive, as trees fill in the creek's shoreline. About 1½ miles from the bridge you encounter a cluster of three islands. Depending on your timetable and appetite, you may wish to use one of the islands as a site for lunch. All three islands are tree-covered, providing shade on a hot day.

Beyond the islands you have 2 miles of fastwater, with a drop of 20 feet. There are no obstacles in this stretch, making paddling a leisurely activity. As you near the second NY 28 bridge you encounter a couple of fast runs with small standing waves. On the south side of the bridge NY 8 intersects NY 28, and together they run south to Poland before separating.

Just below the bridge West Canada splits around a large island. The right channel is the deeper. In the next ½ mile the creek loops to the right and heads south, passing under the NY 8/28 bridge. Just below the bridge the velocity picks up for about a ¼-mile run.

End/Fishing access and parking area   Soon you are passing Poland on your left (it is mostly hidden by trees). A slow bend to your right and ½ mile more of paddling brings you to an abandoned railroad bridge next to Old State Road bridge. West Canada straightens and widens below the bridge as it flows in a more southerly direction. It is a mile from Old State Road bridge to your take-out spot on the left at the creek's edge, just above a fairly sharp bend where the stream is slow, wide, and deep.

Alternate Canoe Routes   West Canada gives you a number of routes to try. The 7-mile stretch from Newport to Middleville is one, and the 6½-mile run from Middleville to Kast Bridge is another, or you can continue below Kast Bridge for 1½ miles to the first dam above Herkimer.

Cincinnati Creek suggests itself for spring and early summer. You can make a day of it by canoeing the 8-mile stretch starting in Remsen and ending just below the junction with West Canada where NY 28 touches West Canada.

There is also the narrow but fast-flowing Feeder Canal, which starts at the Trenton Falls dam and flows south 6 miles to empty into Ninemile Creek (see Trip 23). The canal passes under several roads, giving you a number of put-in and take-out points.

Ninemile Creek

Described Trip:
Stittville to River Road bridge
7 miles
Intermediate at medium or low water
Advanced at medium high water
Expert at high water

Access Points	Interval Distance	Drop and (Gradient)	Trip Time	Water Conditions	Obstacles
South Trenton					
	3¼ miles	247' (77)	1 hr.	Fast, rapids	Barbed wire
Glass Factory Road bridge					
	1	33' (33)	¼	Fast, rapids	Barbed wire
Fox Road bridge (Holland Patent)					
	1	30' (30)	¼	Fast, riffles	Barbed wire
Miller Road bridge					
	1	20' (20)	¼	Fast, riffles	Barbed wire
NY 291 bridge					
	½	*20' (40)*	*7 min.*	*Fast, rapids*	*None*
Mill Street bridge (Stittville)					
	2	30' (15)	½	*Fast, rapids, riffles, ledges*	Barbed wire
Rostiser Road bridge					
	1¼	20' (16)	¼	*Fast, rapids, drops, ledges*	None
1st Richie Road bridge					
	2¼	30' (13)	½	*Fast, rapids, chutes, drops*	None
2nd Richie Road bridge					
	1	5' (5)	¼	*Fast, ledges, riffles*	None
River Road bridge					
	½	5' (10)	10 min.	Moderately fast	*None*
Jct. Barge Canal					
	¼	5' (20)	5 min.	Flat	*Dam*
Jct. Mohawk River					

USGS (7.5') Maps: Newport, South Trenton, Oriskany.

NINEMILE CREEK

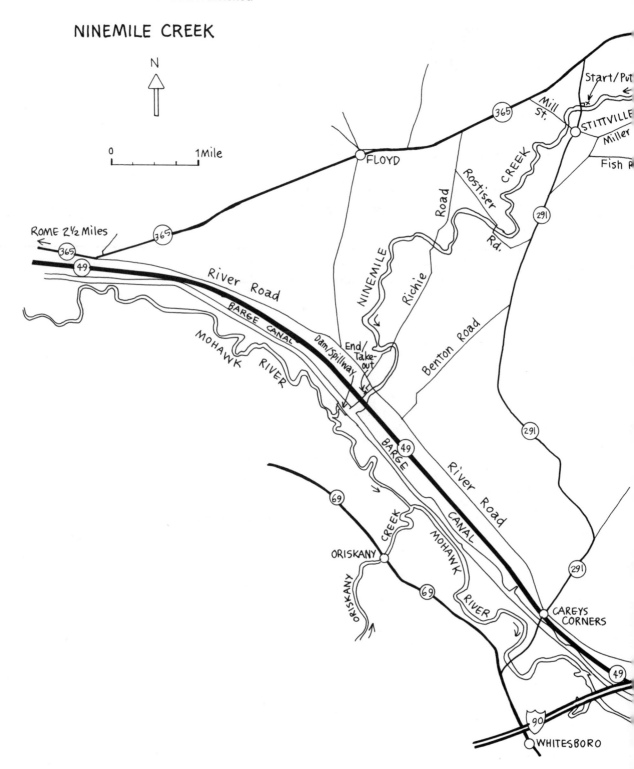

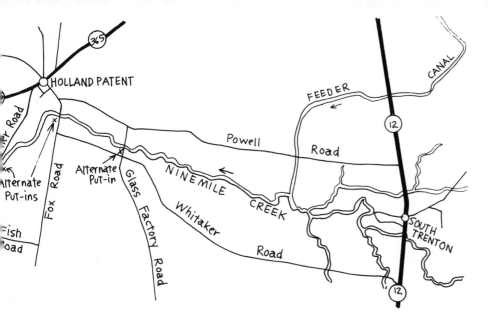

As far as its name is concerned, Ninemile Creek might have an identity crisis. There are a couple other creeks named "Ninemile" in the central New York region; one is southwest of Syracuse, and another is southwest of Oswego. So when one is referring to Ninemile Creek, specific denotation is necessary: this is the creek that lies 6½ miles east of Rome, and runs south from Holland Patent to the Mohawk River.

But when it comes to the creeks' scenic qualities and canoeing characteristics, the identity problem disappears. Swift is its name, and beauty its champion.

It is a fast-moving stream from beginning to end. Ninemile's water rushes, tumbles, and races over and through what appears to be an endless series of shelves, ledges, drops, chutes, and runs. The creek drops 790 feet between its origin in the highlands, 25½ miles to the east, and its terminus at the Barge Canal. This gives Ninemile an impressive gradient of 30, although much of the drop is found in the upper, noncanoeable reaches of the creek.

Even in its wider, canoeable lower portion, which runs from Stittville to the creek's junction with the Barge Canal, Ninemile drops 85 feet in a 7-mile course for a gradient of 12. Translated, this means that on Ninemile you move; it also means you've got to stay alert, know how to read fast water, and keep your eyes on the creek at all times.

Most importantly, however, it means that Ninemile is an exciting stream to paddle—providing you are an experienced canoeist. In early spring when Ninemile is running full with the first meltoff the stream is in the whitewater category, and no one but advanced and expert canoeists ought to be on it. In late spring and early summer when the water is at a medium or even low stage, the intermediate canoeist can give this creek a try.

Access   Several paved roads cross Ninemile at various points between Holland Patent and the Barge Canal, giving easy access for launching or taking out.

River Road crosses Ninemile at the lower end, and can be used to reach your take-out spot. Follow NY 365 east out of Rome. About 2½ miles east of Rome the road forks, with NY 365 bearing to the left and River Road to the right. Take the latter for 3.6 miles. Just before you reach the bridge crossing Ninemile, turn off to the right into a large parking lot. A short dirt road leads to a broad beach area fronting the creek on its west side. This is the take-out point.

The suggested put-in is found where NY 291 crosses Ninemile, immediately north of the hamlet of Stittville. From your take-out site drive northwest a short distance on River Road before turning right onto Richie Road. Richie Road crosses Ninemile twice before intersecting NY 365. Go right on NY 365 and drive northeast a mile to Mill Street. Turn right and follow Mill Street across Ninemile into Stittville. In Stittville turn left on NY 291 and drive a brief distance to the spot where the highway crosses Ninemile. There is a state-constructed fishing access (and parking) area on the northeast side of the bridge. A few short steps bring you to the creek edge for an easy put-in.

The Creek   Ninemile has a number of unusual attributes. One, of course, is the pitch that makes it one of the liveliest streams in central New York. Another is its relatively high water level.

The creek always has enough water, even during long dry periods when other nearby streams are on the scratchy side and dropping. The reason is found in the big assist that Ninemile gets from its cousin, West Canada Creek (see Trip 22), which lies several miles to the northeast.

If you travel 1½ miles west of South Trenton you'll see a good volume of water pouring into Ninemile from a feeder canal. This canal originates 5½ miles to the north at West Canada Creek, in the hamlet of Trenton Falls. The canal was constructed around the time of World War I to divert water from West Canada Creek, via Ninemile Creek, to the Barge Canal. The benefactors of this aquatic rerouting are the happy canoeists who run Ninemile.

Ninemile originates on the west side of Tanner Hill at 1,200 feet elevation, just a scant 3 miles from West Canada Creek. It ends at the Barge Canal at an elevation of 420 feet. From Tanner Hill, Ninemile flows westward to South Trenton and Holland Patent, picking up water from a half dozen streamlets and brooks on the way. Its big water source, of course, is the feeder canal.

At Holland Patent, Ninemile alters its course by heading in a southwesterly direction past Stittville, the only sign of civilization in the creek's lower section. It flows through what is predominately a rural setting. Pastureland for milk cattle surrounds the creek's upper reaches, with fields running to the creek's edge.

Because this is pastureland, barbed wire fencing runs across the creek. So be on the lookout. At the time of this writing, two such fences were stretched across the creek within one 2-mile stretch below Stittville. The creek below this stretch was clear.

Ninemile has been doing what all streams do—deepening its channel—for a long time. In the lower section the creek has eaten its way through soft shale to

Pausing to check gear.

more resistant bedrock. Much of the creek bottom in this section is made up of this rock, which lies in long flat shelves and ledges.

The cuts into shale are impressively deep, and form what almost look like gorges. Because of the land's pitch, the cuts are usually found on one side of the creek. Even so, the cliff walls run straight up as high as four or five stories. Growing out of the cliff's face are cedars and spruces, and sometimes the face is covered with a solid blanket of plants, producing a Japanese effect.

You will also find that the lower section contains a number of rock gardens of large and small boulders through which you must pick your course with care. That's part of the challenge of running a fast stream.

The Trip
Start/NY 291 bridge
at Stittville

A barbed wire fence stretches across the creek just above your launching point. Although there is no problem getting the canoe launched, the water is already running fast, and the current picks up speed in the short stretch between the NY 291 bridge and Mill Street bridge.

Just before you reach the latter, the creek drops a few feet. The water turns into rapids just as the creek bends sharply to the right and passes under the bridge, giving you something between a chute and a run. For the next ¼ mile the creek is fairly flat, but filled with boulders. This calmness soon gives way to an acceleration in the current as the creek drops another 10 feet within the next ¼ mile, resulting in more small rapids and fast runs.

It will drop another 10 feet before you reach Rostiser Road bridge—20 feet in less than 2 miles, meaning that much of what you are paddling is low rapids and small ledges. You'll encounter small stream islands that split the creek channel. Ninemile is predominately a lefthanded creek; the deepest channels are usually found on the left side of the islands.

About a mile downstream from Stittville you reach your first barbed wire fence, and ½ mile farther on you meet the second. You never know if fences will be there after a spring runoff—farmers may replace washed-out wire, or they may fence elsewhere on the creek. So look carefully. Over-stream wire fences are hard to see.

As you approach Rostiser Road bridge, you enter the first shale rock gorge area, with cedars clinging precariously to the cliff face. After you pass the bridge the shale cliff continues on the right for more than ¼ mile, but it gives way to flatter land on the left. The creek, which has been flowing eastward from the bridge, now makes a sharp bend to the left and races southward for ¼ mile to another cliff rising abruptly on the left.

The water is fast, the rapids appear to be almost continuous, and one chute follows another for an exciting run to the cliff edge, where the creek veers to the right in an elbow-turn. Ahead is the first of two Richie Road bridges and another set of rapids; between Rostiser Road and Richie Road bridges—1¼ miles —the creek drops 30 feet for a gradient of almost 30, making this the fastest part of the 7-mile trip.

End/River Road bridge

Below the bridge Ninemile slows a bit, but not much, as it makes a slow turn to return to a southeasterly course. The creek drops another 30 feet before it reaches the second Richie Road bridge, 2¼ miles downstream, but this time with a gradient of only about 10. Just before you reach the bridge, however, rapids again appear, and the creek narrows into a chute. The next mile is a trifle slower, allowing you to catch your breath. Then, just before you reach River Road bridge, the current speeds up, and you run through a stretch of small scallop waves as you ferry across the stream, under the bridge, to your take-out spot on the shallow side.

Alternate Canoe Routes

One alternate possibility is to run the middle section of the creek between Glass Factory Road bridge and the NY 291 bridge at Stittville. Do this in early spring when the creek is up. Barbed wire may be found along here, unless the runoff has washed out the fencing.

Two other routes are worth trying—the Barge Canal and the Mohawk River. For the Barge trip, put in at the River Road bridge and paddle south on Ninemile to its junction with the Barge. Here you can canoe northwest toward Rome, or southeast toward Utica. If you take the latter course you can take out at Careys Corners bridge, 3¼ miles down from the Barge junction.

For the Mohawk trip, carry around the dam on the south side of the Barge Canal, across from its junction with Ninemile. Continue downstream a short distance to the creek's junction with the Mohawk River. You can paddle downriver for 4½ miles and take out at the NY 291 bridge.

24

Mohawk River (Upper)/Delta Lake

Described Trip:
North Western to Delta Lake State Park
3 miles
Novice at medium water
Intermediate at medium high water

Access Points	Interval Distance	Drop and (Gradient)	Trip Time	Water Conditions	Obstacles
Hillside					
	0.8 mile	19' (19)	½ hour	Racy, rapids	None
Hillside Road bridge					
	0.8	34' (34)	½	Fast, runs	None
North Western					
	2.5	*33' (13)*	*¾*	*Runs, riffles*	*None*
Westernville					
	0.8	*18' (18)*	*½*	*Slow, flat*	*None*
Reservoir					
	5.0	*0' (0)*	*2*	*Flat*	*None*
Delta Lake State Park launching site					
	0.8	21' (21)	½	Racy, runs	None
Bridge at Rome Fish Hatchery					
	2.0	17' (8)	¾	Fast	None
Ridge Mills bridge					
	1.6	9' (6)	¾	Moderate	None
Floyd Avenue bridge					
	0.8	9' (9)	½	Flat	None
Junior high school					

USGS (7.5') Maps: Point Rock, Lee Center, Northwestern, Westernville, Rome.

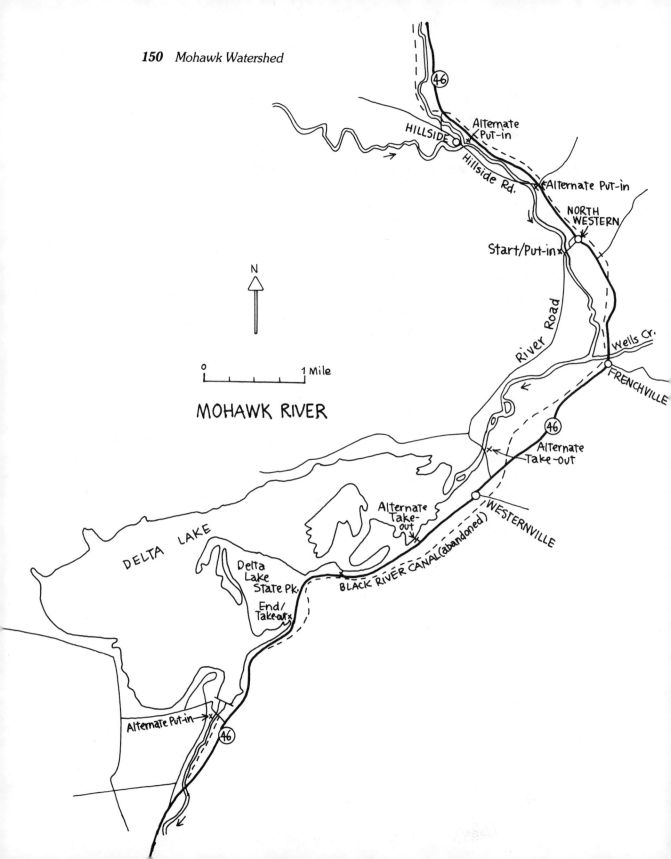

MOHAWK RIVER

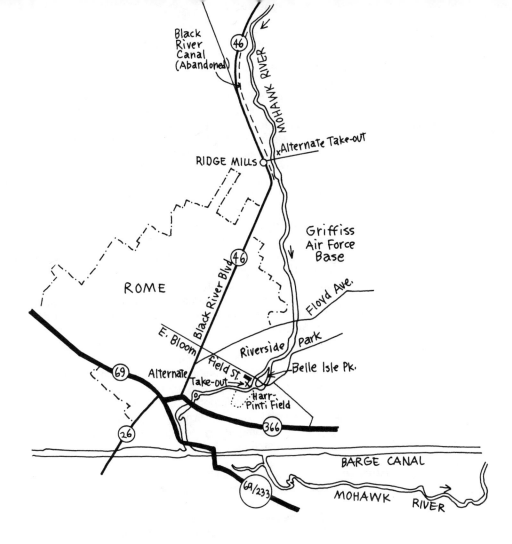

In its upper reaches where the Mohawk River is still young and not very disciplined, you find a spunky stream displaying all the vigor that goes with fastwater—racing down runs and tumbling over drops. This is the Mohawk which canoeists know, a river which, like all young things, is rushing to get somewhere—in the Mohawk's case, to that long, wide, and famous east-west migration route known as the Mohawk Valley, which runs from Rome to Albany.

Once the Mohawk reaches the valley, which it does at the south edge of Rome, it becomes subdued and staid in its movements as, perhaps, befits a more mature river. This is the river that motorists see as they drive along the New York Thruway.

Named after the most easterly Indian tribe of the Iroquoian-speaking Five Nations, the Mohawk was an important transportation route for centuries before the white man came to New York. It remains so now, even though much of today's traffic is made up of pleasure boats.

The city of Rome lies astride an ancient water route that links the Atlantic Ocean with the Great Lakes. On the city's east side is the Mohawk River which eventually feeds its water into the Hudson. On the west side is Wood Creek, a small stream flowing west into Oneida Lake and then into Oswego River, forming a passage to Lake Ontario.

Between the two is level ground, making a portage of about three miles in spring. It was called Trow Plat by the Dutch, and the Oneida Carry by the British. This famous carry permitted the Indians and, later, traders and travelers to journey from the mouth of the Hudson to Canada and back.

To protect the carry the British built several forts during the French and Indian War (1754-63). During the Revolutionary War the colonists occupied the carry, rebuilding Fort Stanwix to hold the area against the British. The fort has recently been reconstructed and is now administered by the National Park Service as a national monument.

Local place names remind us that in the late 1700's this was the western frontier. The town of Western was created in 1797 from the town of Steuben, and soon after that the hamlets of Westernville and North Western were founded.

Along the upper stretches of the Mohawk can be found the remains of the famous Black River Canal with its incredible 109 locks that lifted boats 1,082 vertical feet in its 120-mile length from Rome to Boonville, and then along the Black River to Carthage. Started in 1837 and completed in 1855, this lateral canal became an important northern link of the Erie Canal. It was officially abandoned in 1922 and is now mostly grassed-in and treed-over. As you drive north from Rome along the Mohawk River you can see the stonework of the locks still standing.

Access   A short trip north from Rome on NY 46 brings you to a number of easy access points on the Mohawk. This upper section is divided by a fairly large impoundment, usually called Delta Lake, but also known as Delta Reservoir.

On the lake's east side is Delta Lake State Park, where a large boat launching site can serve as your take-out point. However, to reach the launching site you must paddle around the entire peninsula on which the park is situated. You can reduce this mileage (in case the wind is up and the lake is whitecapping) by taking out on the northern edge of the park where NY 46 runs along the lake edge. There are several good spots to be found here. The park, with over a hundred campsites, makes an ideal place for a weekend campout, should you want to canoe the river both above and below the lake.

Several put-in spots suggest themselves. In spring, when the water level is up, the bridge at Hillside, a small community of eight houses, is a good choice. Hillside Road bridge, .8 mile downriver, is another put-in spot. The most popular place is the River Road bridge at the hamlet of North Western. From here to Delta Lake is about 3 miles in moderately fast water.

The River   Topography and nomenclature have almost obscured the source of the Mohawk. About 27 miles northwest of Rome, just below an uninhabited crossroad called Russian Settlement and marked only by a graveyard, is a pond out of which flows the water that eventually becomes the Mohawk.

Delta Lake.

This small stream soon disappears in a swamp. On the south side of the swamp another small stream appears called Lyman Brook, which flows south through Point Rock State Forest. There it meets Egger Brook, to form the West Branch of the Mohawk. The water now flows eastward, past the hamlet of West Branch where it meets the East Branch, combining to form, finally, the Mohawk River proper. At this point it disappears into a craggy, inaccessible cut in the Haynes Hill area. Five miles downstream at Hillside it reappears as a canoe-able stream.

The Mohawk now races southward past North Western and Westernville only to switch from fastwater to flatwater as it enters the 4-mile-long Delta Lake. If you can switch both your interest and your gear, Delta Lake is ideal for canoe sailing.

Below the dam at the south end of Delta Lake the Mohawk returns to its former fast character, only wider and more robust. The run from here to the center of Rome is a popular one; an outfitter called "Canoes Along the Mohawk" rents canoes at a spot just below the dam.

From the dam the Mohawk continues south, finally entering the city limits of Rome and hugging the city's eastern edge. The setting, surprisingly, retains its rural look even in the city because the river flows through a series of parks in which trees line the riverbanks.

Below the second dam in Rome, the Mohawk flows into the man-made Barge Canal for one last disappearing act which lasts about ¼ mile. Then it emerges as a small stream, quickly growing to its former size as it takes the Barge overflow waters, and maintaining its own independent existence apart from the Barge well past Utica.

The Trip
Start/North Western bridge

If you put in just north of the bridge at North Western you can run a chute on the other side of the bridge; otherwise you have to put in on the south side, where a short flat stretch quickly gives way to fastwater with small standing waves. About ⅔ of the next 3 miles is made up of runs, riffles, and glides—fastwater for fun, but not so swift as to overwhelm the novice.

The runs and glides follow a straight course, making the passage over the drops easy to handle. About ¾ mile downstream you encounter your first bend. The water divides, flowing around a small island, races down a moderate chute, and then turns to the right.

A short distance downstream you pick up the water of Wells Creek, flowing in from Frenchville on NY 46 to your left. The next mile is straight water mixed with a series of riffles and glides, as the Mohawk hurries through a farm valley. Several farms can be seen on both sides of the relatively open valley; cattle are usually grazing in the fields beside the river.

End/Delta Lake State Park or NY 46

You encounter two more river islands; the channel is found by bearing to the right. Just ahead is the Westernville bridge. Once past this bridge, the water slows and flattens. From here to your take-out point it is flatwater canoeing. If you take out at the park's boat launching site it is a 4-mile paddle. To shorten the distance you need only paddle ½ mile to the first alterate take-out next to NY 46. There is another take-out spot, also next to NY 46, farther down the lake.

Alternate Canoe Routes

A popular route is the 5-mile trip from Delta Lake dam to Rome. A good take-out point is the Harr-Pinti playfield or, across the river, the George Staley Junior High School on East Bloomfield Street. The school's parking area (in the rear) is only about 100 feet from the river. The playfield and school are 7 blocks east of Black River Boulevard (NY 46) in Rome.

Sections of the Mohawk below Rome can also be canoed. There are a number of put-in points along the river, allowing you to canoe to Utica and beyond.

25

Oriskany Creek

Described Trip:
Norton Avenue bridge (Clinton) to
Oriskany dam
11 miles
Intermediate at low water
Advanced at medium high water

Access Points	Interval Distance	Drop and (Gradient)	Trip Time	Water Conditions	Obstacles
Oriskany Falls					
	4½ miles	260' (58)	1½ hrs.	Narrow, fast rapids	Debris
Deansboro bridge					
	3½	150' (43)	1¼	Narrow, fast, rapids chutes	Rocks, steps
Farmers Mills bridge					
	3¼	70' (22)	1¼	Fast, rapids, riffles	Rocks
NY 412 bridge (Clinton)					
	1½	20' (13)	¾	Fast, riffles, runs, chutes	Rocks, steps
Norton Ave. bridge (Clinton)					
	1½	*40' (26)*	*¾*	*Fast, riffles, low rapids*	*None*
Kirkland bridge					
	1¼	*10' (8)*	*¾*	*Fast, riffles*	*Some rocks*
Clark Mills bridge					
	2	*30' (15)*	*1*	*Fast, low rapids, runs, riffles*	*None*
Bell Road bridge					
	½	*10' (20)*	*¼*	*Fast, riffles, runs*	*None*
Walesville bridge					
	2	*20' (10)*	*1*	*Fast, riffles, runs, low rapids*	*Some rocks*
Colemans Mills bridge					
	2	*10' (5)*	*1*	*Fast, low rapids, riffles*	*Some rocks*
Oriskany dam					
	½	*20' (40)*	*¼*	*Fast, riffles, runs*	*None*
Oriskany bridge					
	1	*20' (20)*	*½*	*Fast riffles, runs*	*None*
Jct. Mohawk					

USGS (7.5') Maps: Munnsville, Oriskany Falls, Clinton, Utica West, Oriskany.

Clearly this is one of central New York's lively streams. It gathers its water in the south from the Susquehanna hills part of central New York's highlands, and then it makes a dash down the escarpment, racing into the Mohawk Valley where—still in high gear—it ends its career at the Mohawk River. In the lower half of its canoeable section, the Oriskany dances most of its way, dropping 10 feet every ½ mile, but in the upper part it literally cascades its way downhill, with a 10-foot drop every ¼ mile.

In spite of the creek's youthful exuberance, it is locally thought of as a link to the past. Its name is closely associated with Oriskany Battlefield, a Revolutionary War memorial landmark. Here on August 6, 1777, a small militia led by General Nicholas Herkimer halted an invasion of British troops, compelling the British to lift the siege of Fort Stanwix (located at what today is Rome), and securing the Continental Army's western flank in New York.

After the Revolutionary War, Oriskany Creek and its near neighbor Sauquoit Creek (which flows into and through Utica) suppled the waterpower that the early settlers needed to bring industrial production to this region. Throughout the nineteenth century, factories and textile mills sprang up along the Oriskany and the Sauquoit. Today, however, that industrial boom and bustle is no more. What remains are a few unused factory buildings and the sleepy villages with names that reflect the past, such as Farmers Mills, Clark Mills, and Colemans Mills.

Nowadays Oriskany looks much as it did before the settlers came. It is known hereabouts as a trout stream, both picturesque and productive, where fishermen can be found from opening day in April to closing day in September.

It is also known as a scenic and exciting stream for central New York canoeists. Like trout fishing, paddling on the Oriskany is generally best in spring and early summer. By midsummer the creek is down, making it thin and scratchy. However, a good solid rain in summer can bring the creek up from several inches to a half foot—for a great summertime fastwater trip.

Access

Along the Oriskany roads seems to be everywhere, several running parallel to the creek for almost its entire length, with a crossing every mile or less, making access to the stream an easy matter.

The recommended take-out spot is at a dam less than ¼ mile south of the village of Oriskany. Oriskany can be reached via NY 69, coming either from Utica on the east or Rome on the west. In the village turn south onto Valley Road, which takes you to the dam. By the dam is a good sized off-road parking area where you can leave pick-up vehicles.

The put-in spot is at the Norton Avenue bridge in Clinton. Norton Avenue runs into the village from the northwest and can be reached via NY 233 south out of Kirkland. The bridge is located in a rural area, and parking is possible along the paved road.

The Creek

As a quiet rivulet, the Oriskany begins its life at an elevation of 1,500 feet on a ridge between Oak Hill and Prospect Hill, about 2½ miles southeast of Munnsville and 32 miles from the creek's terminus at the Mohawk River (400 feet elevation). Within this distance, the Oriskany drops 1,100 feet for an impressive gradient of 34.

ORISKANY CREEK

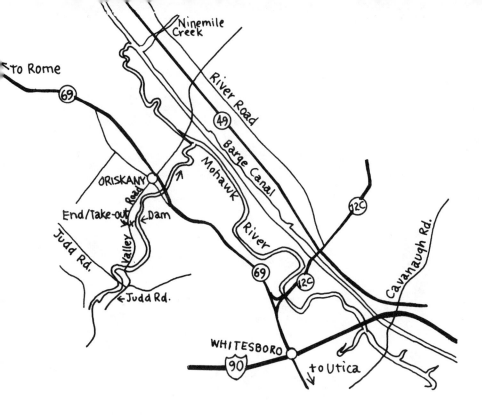

At its start the Oriskany flows south for several miles, but before reaching NY 20 it turns abruptly northeast to pass through Solsville and Oriskany Falls. It then swings even more to the north as it starts down the slope toward the Mohawk Valley, and as it races downhill it becomes more robust, gathering water from Buckley Mill, Big Creek, Turkey Creek, and a dozen other unnamed streams. By the time it gets to Farmers Mills, the Oriskany has reached a canoeable level.

The creek will accommodate paddlers from novice through advanced, but on different sections and at different times of the year. When the creek is full with the early spring runoff, running the canoeable portion which starts at Farmers Mills is a white-knuckle, teeth-clenching experience, for advanced paddlers only. Later, in early summer, the intermediate paddler can try his or her skill on the downstream section starting at Clinton. And the short, 1-mile section from Oriskany to the Mohawk River can usually be handled by the novice during the summer.

For most of the canoeing season, the 12-mile section starting at Clinton is racy, with a current ranging from fast to swift. In this section the drop is 180 feet for a speedy gradient of 15. Here the water races over small drops and steps, down short chutes, and through a few rock gardens. When the water is medium high the bowman has to have a sharp eye and fast reflexes, to keep the craft away from canoehungry boulders. As the water drops to low, water travel becomes less demanding, but also a bit more scratchy, requiring a certain amount of dragging in the thin portions.

Doing some bird watching on the Oriskany.

The area along the Oriskany is filled with well-kept, attractive homes interspersed with barns and farmland. Every couple of miles the creek passes through or near a small village or hamlet, but in spite of this population density the countryside looks more rural than suburban, and more forested than settled. Once you start downstream, all signs of civilization disappear behind thick clusters of trees that line the banks.

The abundance of wildlife found along this stream is a pleasant surprise—more birds and beasts than you ever encounter in a wilderness. In one day's trip we saw two dozen mallard ducks, scores of kingfishers, four redtail hawks (three circling together on the thermals), one great horned owl, several great blue herons, three green herons, an American bittern, a colony of bank swallows, and a groundhog perched high on the lip of a cliff, surveying his domain.

The Trip
Start/Norton Avenue bridge (Clinton)

It is a short, easy descent to the creek's edge on the northeast side of the bridge. Once in the water you have a flat stretch of about 100 yards before you encounter your first riffles. The creek here runs, as it does in the other sections, past tree-lined banks and through an attractive rural landscape.

Farther downstream the current picks up for a short, bouncy run; within ¼ mile the creek has dropped 10 feet, and in the next ½ mile it drops another 10. In this section you are treated to several stretches of low rapids and fast runs.

You are now approaching Kirkland, but from the creek you are hardly aware of the town's presence; trees block out the few houses situated along NY 5. On the southeast side of the Kirkland (NY 5) bridge is a public fishing access parking lot which can serve as an alternate put-in spot.

As you approach the bridge you pass through another stretch of riffles, and then you have a short, smooth stretch which quickly gives way to another run with low rapids and small standing waves. Within the next ½ mile the Oriskany wiggles a bit, flattening out as it bends to the right to run alongside a railroad track for ¼ mile before swinging to the left again. Here it picks up water from two brooks, one coming in from the right and another from the left.

The stream drops another 10 feet through a section of riffles and low rapids Ahead on your right you see an old factory building through the trees, indicating you are approaching Clark Mills. Soon you pass under the Clark Mills bridge, and shortly thereafter you go under a railroad bridge, heading for more riffles and runs.

The creek then slows somewhat as it moves into a low, wooded, swampy area. A half mile brings you to Bell Road bridge where the land on both sides rises sharply to form a narrow neck through which the creek flows, and another ½ mile of fastwater finds you at Stone Road bridge in Walesville.

Downstream from the bridge there is a smooth stretch, and then a nice drop of several feet in the form of a chute. A half mile farther on, you see Deans Creek coming in on the left. The Oriskany is now running flat but fast, and soon you hear the first sounds of auto traffic ahead. You are approaching the New York Thruway (I-90). The creek parallels the Thruway a short distance, then turns left to pass under the Thruway bridge.

A quarter mile stretch of riffles brings you to Old Judd Road bridge at Colemans Mills. The next mile continues to be fast, with a nice mix of riffles, low rapids, runs, and races. As you reach Judd Road bridge the Oriskany bends to the right, passes under the bridge, and swings sharply to the left to form a loop that brings you in a half circle to Valley Road bridge—the last bridge before your take-out.

Just before you reach Valley Road bridge, the Oriskany drops again through a rock garden, rapids, and a chute. A turn to the right puts you under the bridge and through another riffle section.

You have come into a narrow valley with the land rising sharply on both sides of the creek. In several bare spots along the righthand hill you'll see a dozen or more holes in the cliff face. These are the homes of bank swallows; you see them darting in and out.

End/Dam south of Oriskany

The creek begins to slow now, as the water is being backed upstream by the dam. Ahead you see several houses on Valley Road, indicating you have reached your take-out spot. The creek has widened and ahead you hear the sound of water pouring over the dam. Pull to your left and take out near the parking area.

Alternate Canoe Routes

There is a short, 1½ mile stretch of moderately fast water from the dam south of Oriskany to the Mohawk River. When you reach the river, canoe upstream on the Mohawk 100 yards to the Valley Road bridge, where you can take out on the southeast side.

Both the Mohawk River and its close neighbor the Barge Canal are close at hand as alternate canoe routes. You can start at the bridge in Oriskany and canoe Oriskany Creek to the Mohawk, then follow the Mohawk downstream 3 miles to the NY 12C bridge. An additional 1½ miles will bring you to the Cavanaugh Road bridge, a little less than a mile northeast of Whitesboro.

26

Old Erie Canal

Described Trip:
Durhamville to New London
9 miles
Novice at medium through high water

Access Points	Interval Distance	Drop and (Gradient)	Trip Time	Water Conditions	Obstacles
Cedar Bay (Dewitt)					
	6½ miles	1' (0)	2¼ hours	Flat	None
Pools Brook Picnic Area					
	3½	0' (0)	1¼	Flat	None
Chittenango bridge					
	6¼	1' (0)	2¼	Flat	None
Canastota					
	5	1' (0)	2	Flat	None
Durhamville					
	3	*2' (1)*	*1*	*Flat*	*None*
Mills Road bridge					
	2	*2' (1)*	*¾*	*Flat*	*None*
Starks Landing bridge					
	2	*0' (0)*	*¾*	*Flat*	*None*
Stacy Basin bridge					
	2	*0' (0)*	*¾*	*Flat*	*None*
New London					
	½	*0' (0)*	*¼*	*Flat*	*None*
Jct. Barge Canal					

USGS (7.5') Maps: Syracuse East, Manilus, Canastota, Oneida, Sylvan Beach, Verona

163

Before you can say that you've canoed central New York you really should paddle the Old Erie Canal. True, mule-hauled packet boats no longer appear on the canal, and you no longer hear the cry, "Low bridge!" from the helmsman. Today what one sees are bikers and joggers on the towpath and, occasionally, a canoeist on the water.

But the Old Erie is still around and still serviceable—meaning that several long sections of the canal, such as the 30-mile stretch from Syracuse to New London, are delightful, canoeable waterways. While it runs a straight course in flat country, the canal is tree-lined for almost its entire distance, as it flows with a moderate current through green-carpeted countryside that is dotted with farms and small hamlets.

Construction on what is now called the Old Erie Canal began on July 4, 1817, and on October 20, 1825 the 363-mile canal—running from New York City to Buffalo—was completed. The digging began in Rome and progressed westward to Salina (now Syracuse), taking advantage of the "long level" (flat land) stretching from Utica to Salina. In 1819, an 89-mile section between Utica and the Seneca River (see Trip 10) was completed. Today 30 miles of this section is still usable.

The original canal was 40 feet wide and 4 feet deep; 83 locks took it over various land levels. When completed, the Erie was the main route between the Atlantic Ocean and the Great Lakes and, of course, the western frontier. It was hailed as one of the foremost engineering feats of its time.

Late in the 19th century, sections of the canal were widened and deepened a few feet for larger canal boats. By the turn of the century, however, railroads were successfully competing with, and then beating, the Erie as the main transportation system across the state. Soon thereafter the state replaced the Erie with the Barge Canal, which made maximum use of existing streams and rivers. The Erie was officially abandoned. Large sections were drained of water; others were filled in and paved over.

But parts of the abandoned canal were left intact. Such sections are found around Rochester, between Rochester and Syracuse, and between Syracuse and Rome. In the 1950's and early 1960's, a drive got underway to clean up the usable sections of the Old Erie and make them into multi-use recreational facilities. The result is today's Old Erie Canal State Park.

New York owns the canal bed and a narrow strip of land on both sides, including, of course, the towpath. Certainly it is not a conventional park, but this narrow, 30-mile piece of land is an ideal facility for hikers, strollers, joggers, bikers, birders, and boaters, who enjoy having mile upon linear mile at their disposal.

There's nothing difficult about becoming physically acquainted with the Old Erie. Just slip your canoe into the canal anywhere along the 30-mile route and paddle away. Becoming historically acquainted with the canal may be slightly more complicated, taking you to nearby libraries and to local canal museums, such as those in Syracuse and Canastota. Both kinds of investigation are recommended.

Access   One of the nice things about the Old Erie is that it can be easily reached at dozens of points along its course, and the state has provided a parking area at each place where a road crosses the canal.

OLD ERIE CANAL

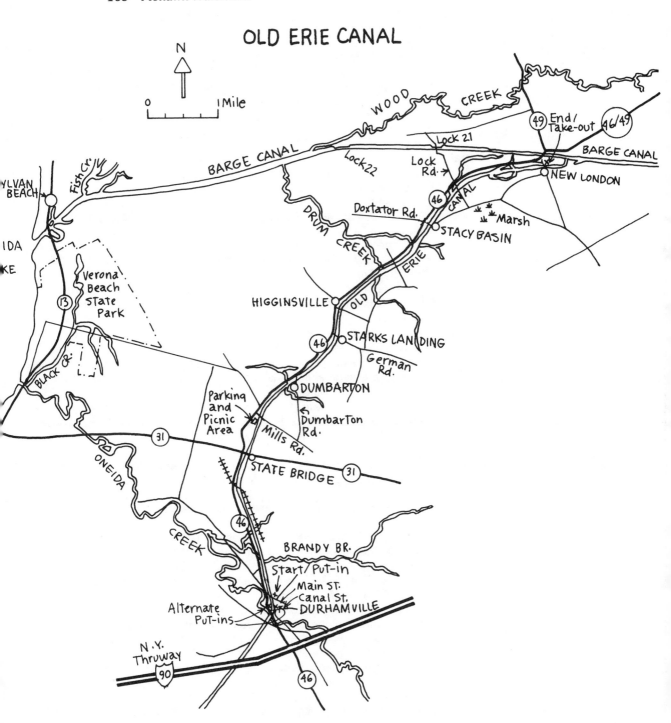

A good take-out spot is at the bridge crossing the canal in the hamlet of New London. The canal continues another ½ mile beyond New London to its junction with the Barge Canal.

An alternate put-in point is at Durhamville where NY 46 crosses the canal. You can put in on the east side of the highway. Several other roads cross the canal in Durhamville. A short distance north of the NY 46 bridge, and a block still farther north is the Main Street bridge, which is the recommended launch point.

The Canal

The water in the canal flows eastward, making this waterway part of the Mohawk River watershed. The current ranges from slow to moderate, with the fastest movement between Durhamville and New London, although the drop is only 5 feet between these two hamlets.

This section of canoeable canal starts at the eastern edge of DeWitt, a suburb of Syracuse, at the point where Butternut Creek crosses under the canal. Here is found one of several original aqueducts built to carry the canal over existing streams. Another aqueduct is two miles to the east, crossing Limestone Creek. Aqueducts are also found over Chittenango Creek, Canaserga Creek, Canastota Creek, and Cowaselon Creek. The one crossing Oneida Creek is of more recent vintage, and is constructed of concrete rather than limestone.

The canal's course from Syracuse to Canastota is straight as a ruler due east. At Canastota, however, it takes a northeasterly course to Durhamville, where it veers even more sharply northward to Starks Landing. From this point the canal swings several degrees to the east, continuing in this direction until it reaches its junction with the Barge Canal.

Along the canal route are found "wide water" sections where the canal is five or six canoe lengths across. In the old days canalers used to turn their boats around in these wide places for their return trips.

The Trip
Start/Durhamville

Probably the best put-in spot is at or near the Main Street bridge in Durhamville. Once you are underway the houses at the northern edge of the village quickly fall behind and disappear. Trees line both sides of the canal, but they are small enough and sufficiently spaced to let you see farm fields beyond them.

NY 46 runs tight against the canal on the lefthand side. Along the highway you'll spot houses or farm buildings from time to time. About ¼ mile north of Durhamville, the canal passes over Brandy Brook flowing from the east and heading for Oneida Creek in the west. Shortly after that, the canal widens to touch the road on its east side.

As the canal slowly narrows it passes over another small, unnamed brook. A half mile farther on, the canal bends to the right, passes under a railroad bridge, and immediately thereafter it flows over another unnamed brook. Houses become more numerous along NY 46, indicating that you are approaching the hamlet of State Bridge and the east-west highway, NY 31.

A half mile more brings you to Mills Road bridge and a possible take-out spot if your schedule includes a lunch break. Adjacent to the intersection of Mills Road and NY 46, there is a large parking area where you'll find picnic tables and shade trees.

View of Erie Canal and towpath.

From Mills Road bridge it is just over ½ mile to Dumbarton Road bridge, and another mile to German Road bridge at Starks Landing, which has a couple of houses to justify its place on the map. Ahead, however, there are more houses on your left, and soon you pass under a bridge at Higginsville. In just over ½ mile an aqueduct takes you over Drum Creek.

End/New London bridge

Another mile brings you to Doxatator Road bridge at Stacy Basin. For the last several miles the canal has been arcing eastward. After Stacy Basin this arc becomes more pronounced as you pass under Lock Road. From here it is a little over a mile to your take-out spot on the west side of the bridge in New London. En route you pass a thickly wooded marshy area on the right and paddle over a couple more unnamed brooks. The half-mile stretch of canal from New London to the Barge Canal is canoeable, but it is weed-filled. However, if you're curious about the canal's terminus, you can paddle to the Barge for a look-see.

Alternate Canoe Routes

Several alternate canal sections suggest themselves, such as the one from Cedar Bay (near Syracuse) to Pools Brook picnic area, and the one from Pools Brook to Canastota. The former runs 6½ miles, and the latter 8½ miles.

At Durhamville you have the opportunity to canoe a 9-mile stretch of Oneida Creek which takes you from Durhamville northwest to Oneida Lake, where it empties at a spot about ½ mile south of Verona Beach State Park (where you can picnic, swim, and hike).

Still another possibility is the Barge Canal. Once you've reached the Barge via the Old Erie, turn left and head west for 7½ miles to the village of Sylvan Beach on Oneida Lake. You can take out on the south shore at the NY 13 bridge.

Glossary

This book has been written as a canoeing guide to central New York streams; it is intended for the use of both beginners and more experienced canoeists. With the beginner particularly in mind, every effort has been made to keep technical terms to a minimum. Where such terms are unavoidable they have been defined either in the text where they occur or in this glossary.

Access or Access Point. The launching or landing site at streamside or lakeside location.

Back country. An unpopulated and distant wildness area in which it is possible to canoe.

Bottom scrapers. Portions of creeks or rivers in which the water is too low to canoe without scraping bottom.

Canoe-paddling. Moving a canoe by means of paddling, in contrast to poling or sailing. See canoe-poling and canoe-sailing.

Canoe-poling. Moving a canoe by use of a wooden or aluminum pole.

Canoe-sailing. Moving a canoe by use of sails.

Canoe Pole. Wood or aluminum pole, 10 to 14 feet in length, used to propel a canoe.

Carry. Same as portage; refers to the movement of canoe and gear around an obstacle such as a dam, or overland between two waterways. Also used to refer to the route taken.

Channel. That section of a stream which is most navigable, or a navigable route around a stream's obstructions, such as rocks.

Chute. Fast-moving water between two obstacles; generally, the combined narrowing of stream and speeding up of water flow as the stream is compressed between two obstructions.

Cruising. A leisurely mode of canoeing or canoe-sailing from place to place, usually on flatwater; similar to floating. See float.

Current. Speed of water flow or rate of flow of a river; slow current means a gentle flow and fast current means a strong flow.

Deadwater. Non-moving water; such water as found in ponds or just above a dam.

Downstream. Direction of water flow in a creek or river; lower section of the stream from the point at which you are canoeing.

Drag. As a verb it means pulling a canoe over extremely shallow spots on a creek or river.

Drop. A sharp pitch or dip in a stream, usually marked by rapids or chute.

Eddy. Slow current or quiet water at variance with the main current, usually found on the downstream side of rocks where water flows in circular fashion; in canoeing an eddy can be used for resting or for moving upstream in the form of "eddy hopping."

Eddy Turn. A fast maneuver executed to allow the canoe to enter or leave an eddy.

Fastwater. Swift-flowing water, usually marked by the presence of rapids.

Ferrying. The movement or propulsion of canoe laterally across the current; to cross a stream. In forward ferry the bow is into the current; in back ferry the stern is into the current.

Flatwater. Refers to water found in lakes or streams in which no rapids exist; also called stillwater or quietwater.

Float. A canoe trip on a stream with relatively flat water; similar to canoe cruising.

Flow. A combination of brooks, creeks, and rivers that make up the geographical drainage system of a particular region; generally identified by the direction of the water flow.

Glide. A smooth, easy flow of water.

Gradient. The average rate of drop in a stream, usually expressed in terms of feet per mile.

Hang-ups. Refers to the extremely shallow

sections of stream in which the canoe is unable to pass without touching bottom, or to rocky sections of riffles or rapids onto which the canoe runs aground.

Haystack. Standing wave at bottom of a strong chute or sluice produced when a fast current strikes a slower current.

Heavy water. A large volume of water in a rapids section with higher than normal amounts of turbulence.

High water. Refers to the water level of a stream that is well above normal level.

Hydraulics. Generally refers to extremely turbulent water associated with rocks and rapids; more specifically, the back roll of water at the bottom of dams or steep chutes. Considered most dangerous.

Launching. The act of placing a canoe into the water to start a trip.

Launch Point. Same as put-in point; the streamside or lakeside location at which the canoe is launched.

Ledge. A stratum of rock which projects into a stream; may restrict or dam the stream's flow. Sometimes hazardous.

Left bank. The left side of the stream when facing downstream.

Lining. The use of line (rope) to guide a canoe downstream through shallow or turbulent water.

Low water. Level of stream's water that is well below normal; water is usually too shallow for good canoeing.

Medium water. The stream's water level that is usually considered normal; in general the level is high enough for a canoe's easy passage.

Meander. A winding course taken by a stream in relatively flat terrain; water flow is usually slow.

Passage. Route of canoe travel; used by canoeist to refer to the best path around obstacles or obstruction.

Pitch. Incline of stream; can be spoken of as the stream's drop or gradient.

Pole. See canoe pole.

Poling. See canoe-poling.

Portage. See carry.

Put-in. See launch point; spot on stream or lake at which canoe is launched.

Quickwater. See fastwater.

Quietwater. See flatwater and stillwater.

Rapids. Flow of fastwater over rocks, usually with enough noise to be heard some distance upstream. Can range from low to heavy rapids. Associated with rapids are waves, haystacks, whitewater, and other forms of turbulence.

Race. A long stretch of fast-moving water without rapids.

Reading the water. Refers to the ability of canoeists to determine downstream water conditions by observing water formation and behavior; employed by canoeists to pick best and safest channel or route.

Reversals. Refers to back-rolling water found at the bottom of dams and steep chutes; since it can entrap both canoe and canoeist it is considered dangerous. See hydraulics.

Riffles. Shallow but swift water flowing over a gravel or sandy bottom, producing small standing waves; also can be called gentle rapids.

Right bank. The right side of the stream when facing downstream.

Rock garden. Expression used by canoeists to refer to a stretch of water filled with large rocks or boulders in which canoeing is difficult; requires tricky maneuvering.

Run. As a noun, refers to a stretch of fast-moving water with rapids that is marked by a fairly steep gradient or pitch but not as steep or as long as a race; as a verb it refers to the act of canoeing a fast-moving stream.

Running. Canoeing fastwater, as in the phrase "river running."

Scalloped waves. A series of small waves characteristic of fastwater flowing between rocks, indicative of a clear, deep channel.

Scouting. Checking an unknown stretch of water downstream before attempting to canoe it.

Scratchy. Water so shallow that the canoe touches bottom or rocks and becomes scratched in passage.

Shuttle. Arrangement of transportation between put-in and take-out points. Refers also to routes taken by all vehicles between these points. In the most common shuttle arrangement, all vehicles are left at the take-out, with one vehicle returning all canoeists to the put-in spot.

Sluice. A narrow channel of water, similar to a chute.

Souse hole. A depression at the bottom of a dam or a steep chute where water rolls back in a circular fashion. See hydraulics.

Snubbing. The technique of slowing or stopping a canoe's momentum with a canoe pole while running downstream.

Standing waves. Gentle or large waves which remain stationary in a section of fast-moving water; also called regular waves. They usually mark a clear channel.

Stairsteps. A series of natural strata (or steps) running downstream in stair-like fashion.

Stillwater. See flatwater and quietwater.

Strainer. Any collection of objects, usually downed trees, acting as an obstacle or obstruction to canoeing, but through which water passes. The flow of water can pull a canoe into the strainer, entrapping both canoe and canoeist. A dangerous hazard.

Swamping. Upsetting the canoe, or having the canoe take on large amounts of water; also called dumping.

Take-out. Location at a streamside or a lakeside where the canoe is landed, usually at the end of a trip.

Thin. Refers to a stream's low water level; usually too shallow for easy canoeing.

Upstream. The section of the stream from which the water flows.

Watershed. The entire region drained by a single river.

Whitewater. Long stretches of extremely fast water marked by white-capped rapids; considerable skill is required to maneuver a canoe in such water.

Wildwater. Long stretches of highly turbulent and dangerous water with extremely powerful currents and filled with heavy rapids, long drops, haystacks, and other violent water characteristics.

Guidebooks from Backcountry Publications

Written for people of all ages and experience, these popular and carefully prepared books feature detailed trail and tour directions, notes on points of interest and natural phenomena, maps and photographs.

Walks and Rambles Series

Walks and Rambles on The Delmarva Peninsula, by Jay Abercrombie $8.95
Walks and Rambles in Westchester (NY) and Fairfield (CT) Counties, by Kaye Anderson $7.95
Walks and Rambles in Rhode Island, by Ken Weber $8.95

Biking Series

25 Bicycle Tours in Maine, by Howard Stone $8.95
25 Bicycle Tours in Vermont, by John Freidin $7.95
25 Bicycle Tours in New Hampshire, by Tom and Susan Heavey $6.95
20 Bicycle Tours in the Finger Lakes, by Mark Roth and Sally Walters $7.95
20 Bicycle Tours in and around New York City, by Dan Carlinsky and David Heim $6.95
25 Bicycle Tours in Eastern Pennsylvania, by Adams and Speicher $7.95

Canoeing Series

Canoe Camping Vermont and New Hampshire Rivers, by Roioli Schweiker $6.95
Canoeing Central New York, by William P. Ehling $9.95
Canoeing Massachusetts, Rhode Island and Connecticut, by Ken Weber $7.95

Hiking Series

50 Hikes in the Adirondacks, by Barbara McMartin $9.95
50 Hikes in Central New York, by William P. Ehling $8.95

50 Hikes in the Hudson Valley, by Barbara McMartin and Peter Kick $9.95
50 Hikes in Central Pennsylvania, by Tom Thwaites $9.95
50 Hikes in Eastern Pennsylvania, by Carolyn Hoffman $9.95
50 Hikes in Western Pennsylvania, by Tom Thwaites $9.95
50 Hikes in Maine, by John Gibson $8.95
50 Hikes in the White Mountains, by Daniel Doan $9.95
50 More Hikes in New Hampshire, by Daniel Doan $9.95
50 Hikes in Vermont, 3rd edition, revised by the Green Mountain Club $8.95
50 Hikes in Massachusetts, by John Brady and Brian White $9.95
50 Hikes in Connecticut, by Gerry and Sue Hardy $8.95
50 Hikes in West Virginia, by Ann and Jim McGraw $9.95

Adirondack Series, by Barbara McMartin

Discover the Adirondacks, 2 $7.95
Discover the South Central Adirondacks $8.95
Discover the Southeastern Adirondacks $8.95
Discover the Central Adirondacks $8.95
Discover the Southwestern Adirondacks $9.95
Discover the Northeastern Adirondacks (summer 1987)
Discover the Eastern Adirondacks (fall 1987)

The above titles are available at bookstores and at certain sporting goods stores or may be ordered directly from the publisher. For complete descriptions of these and other guides, write: Backcountry Publications, P.O. Box 175, Woodstock, VT 05091.